death of King Harold, as depicted in the Bayeux Tapestry.
original linen tapestry, which tells the story of the Norman
quest, is 230ft long and 20in deep.

AF333962

vast supplies of timber. Streams were dammed, which created hammer ponds to provide the water needed to drive the hammers and bellows. All types of ironwork were produced but the main output of the foundries was cannons for home use and export and the industry brought great wealth and prosperity to the county for two centuries. All the cannons used at the time of the Armada were made in Sussex.

By the 18th century technology had advanced to the position where iron smelting could be perfected using coal and added to the fact that Sussex iron ore was having to be mined at lower levels, production moved to the Midlands. The last forge closed in Sussex around 1810.

Martello Towers: Seventy-four towers were erected along the south eastern coastline between 1805 and 1812. The towers were most numerous in the 16-mile stretch between Hastings and Eastbourne, where 31 were erected and there were 12 in the Bexhill area alone.

They were erected to resist the feared Napoleonic invasion and were nicknamed 'bulldogs' by the French. They were positioned to provide total cover by gun-fire and the tapered shape was designed to deflect cannon shot. The thick walls were bonded by a specially prepared lime mortar and a 24lb gun was placed on the roof. To further confuse the French there was no doorway at ground level. Entry was via a movable ladder to the first floor.

The name derives from the tower at Mortella Point in Corsica, which had provided strong resistance to British forces in 1794. This building was the inspiration for the British design.

Most of the towers have now gone, but there are several survivors in the area. Examples can be found at Rye Harbour, Normans Bay and Pevensey Bay.

Smuggling: The illicit trade began as long ago as the 13th century when Edward I imposed a duty on exported wool and later on many other substances, including wines, spirits, tobacco and tea. Initially there was no proper enforcement of the system and it was not until the 17th century that preventive vessels patrolled the coast and a land-based customs service came into operation to make it harder for the smuggler to escape detection.

However, many customs officials were open to bribery and smugglers were mostly able to carry on their illicit trade unhindered. Even those that were caught were seldom punished. Many of the magistrates and officers appointed to enforce the law were involved in smuggling themselves. Even some of the clergy turned a blind eye to it. Most of the population were involved in some way or another and enjoyed the benefits of cheap goods.

The area has many smuggling stories. Author Rudyard Kipling *(see Burwash)* named them 'the gentlemen' and although their image is often painted as romantic, in fact many were ruthless, vicious men, who thought nothing of beating or even murdering informers who intended to testify against them.

By the mid 19th century a more efficient coastguard service took over the coastal patrols and high rewards were offered for information leading to the conviction of smugglers. Also the duty payable on many goods was lowered and on some substances abolished altogether. This combination caused public opinion to swing against the smuggler for the first time and smuggling began its demise.

Royal Coat of Arms: The displaying of the monarch's coat of arms in English churches was introduced by Henry VIII, to denote his control. The custom continued until Cromwellian times when the majority were removed and destroyed. There are several fine surviving examples within the area.

Battle Abbey gatehouse

Battle

Situated six miles from Hastings on the A2100 is the town of Battle, scene of the conflict which shaped the course of English history in 1066 — the Battle of Hastings. The battle was so named because Hastings was then the nearest centre of population.

Battle is an essential part of the 1066 story and the beautifully picturesque town is a popular all year venue for tourists from every part of the world. Although steeped in history, Battle today is a thriving place with over 150 shops, six public houses and many places of interest. There are ample car parking facilities and the best way to see the town and feel its atmosphere is on foot.

And so to the history. Tradition says that William the Conqueror made a vow before the Battle of Hastings, that if victorious he would found a monastery to the glory of God. However, it is now generally accepted that this vow was made four years after his victory, when the papal authorities insisted the Normans do penance for the loss of life incurred during the conquest of England and William ordered a monastery to be established as an act of atonement for the slaughter.

Battle Abbey, dedicated to the warrior monk, St Martin de Bello, was the result and the high altar of the church was placed on the spot where King Harold fell. Building started in 1070 and the abbey church was consecrated in 1094, in the presence of the Conqueror's son, King William Rufus.

As the Benedictine abbey grew in stature, the post of abbot held great power. Under royal decree all land within one-and-a-half miles of the high altar (the leuga) came under his total jurisdiction. Mitred abbots became members of the House of Lords and entertained many distinguished visitors, from royalty downwards. This state of affairs continued until the dissolution of the monastaries by Henry VIII in 1538, when the last incumbent, Abbot John Hammond, surrendered his position.

Battle, Rye
& the villages

THE OUTSKIRTS OF HASTINGS & BEXHILL

<table>
<tr><td colspan="2">Contents</td></tr>
<tr><td>General information</td><td>2</td></tr>
<tr><td>To Battle and the west</td><td>4</td></tr>
<tr><td>To the north</td><td>23</td></tr>
<tr><td>Eastwards to Rye</td><td>34</td></tr>
<tr><td>Map</td><td>Inside back cover</td></tr>
</table>

This booklet is a brief introduction to the towns and villages of a corner of East Sussex which is very special to me; the beautiful area immediately surrounding the coastal towns of Hastings and Bexhill, where the Southern Forest Ridges merge with the Low Weald and form what is popularly known as 1066 Country.

From the delightful 'olde worlde' town of Rye in the east, to the landing place of the Normans in the west at Pevensey; the charming villages of Burwash and Bodiam to the north and the birthplace of the nation and scene of the famous conflict of 1066 — Battle. There is so much of interest.

In this part of the county you will find everything that is best about Sussex, be it fine architecture, historic castles, ancient churches or just the wonderful views. It is an area rich in history and natural beauty. From the early Roman occupation, to the Battle of Hastings, through to the Napoleonic Wars and the Second World War, this part of England has been to the fore and each period in history has left its indelible mark.

Hopefully the booklet will be of interest to both visitor and resident alike and was prompted by the success of two similar publications, *An Introduction to Hastings and St Leonards* and *An Introduction to Bexhill-on-Sea*.

The object is to help the reader discover a little of the history of the area, the modern day attractions and perhaps some of the less obvious points of interest. For convenience, I have split the booklet into three sections, west, north and east and Hastings is used as a starting and finishing point for the journeys. The map on the inside back cover will hopefully give you a rough directional guide to the places mentioned and show you the quickest access, but please don't be afraid to be flexible and use the minor roads as well. There are no set rules to discovering the beautiful countryside of East Sussex! It's far more exciting exploring the lesser-used routes and is certainly a better way of obtaining the true 'feel' of the area. Most of the villages and towns are well signposted. You won't get lost!

Descriptions in the booklet are brief, but hopefully most of the relevant details, both historic and otherwise, are mentioned. Should the visitor require further detailed information there is a wealth of literature on all aspects of the county and many of the places mentioned have excellent comprehensive guides and tourist information centres.

I hope this booklet gives you a flavour of my part of East Sussex, my home for many years and in my view one of the loveliest parts of the country. If you are a visitor to the area, have an enjoyable stay — *Geoff Hutchinson,*

Acknowledgements
My thanks to the Hastings Reference Library, Hastings Museum, The Hastings and Bexhill Tourist Information Offices, Keith Fitz Hugh, Jan Roadnight and all the many helpful folk around the villages who have contributed information and advice.

General information . . .

Geography: Hastings is situated at the southernmost point of the Southern Forest Ridges. It is surrounded by beautiful undulating countryside and the rivers Brede, Tillingham and Rother form wide valleys to the east.

There is much farming land in the area and hops are grown in some places, although not as extensively as in the past. Many fine old oasthouses, now converted to dwellings, are reminders of this once booming trade.

To the east of Hastings, splendid sandstone cliffs line the coast and merge with the open shingle expanses of Pett Level and Rye Harbour. The glorious Camber Sands, extend eastwards to the Kent border.

To the west is the modern coastal resort of Bexhill, which adjoins the Low Weald, at the marshes of Pevensey Level.

Many of the towns and villages mentioned in this booklet have things in common. The following paragraphs explain these recurring themes.

The Domesday Book: This comprehensive survey of life in Norman times was the product of the curiosity and powerful will of William the Conqueror.

William I was one of the most forceful and able kings ever to rule England and in 1085 he sent his officials to every part of England, except the extreme north, to make a survey of all estates and manors in the country. Nothing was missed; the names of the landowners, acreage, buildings, livestock, servants — and their value. The survey was so thorough, it was compared to the Last Day of Judgement, and hence became known as The Domesday Book. From its conception to fruition, the survey took under two years to complete.

The Domesday Book has remained as proof of ancient landholding, rights and boundaries, through the years and is still considered admissible legal evidence.

William the Conqueror did not have long to digest the vast amount of information contained in the survey. He died in battle at Rouen in 1087.

The Cinque Ports: The early history is vague, but it is reasonable to assume that the five original ports of Hastings, Romney, Hythe, Dover and Sandwich, were first given individual charters before being unified into a Confederation. Tradition says the original charters were granted by Edward the Confessor in the eleventh century. Later Rye and Winchelsea were added, when the organisation was renamed The Confederation of Cinque Ports and the Two Antient Towns. The purpose of the organisation was to provide defence against invasion from the Continent, to convey the king and his forces overseas and support any fighting campaign.

In 1278 the duties of the Cinque Ports were legally established by Royal Charter, when each port was given the task of providing an agreed number of ships for the king's navy. The fleet of 57 ships was the only English navy until the 15th century and was the forerunner of The Royal Navy. In return for their services, the ports were granted certain privileges.

The Sussex Iron Industry: In the 14th century the harbours, which had proved so vital to trade, had started to erode and were being ruined by silting. Business was lost to the Kentish ports and Sussex experienced decline.

However, by the late 15th century, the production of iron had brought a new prosperity. Many villages and towns, previously farming areas, became cogs in the mighty Sussex iron industry. Sussex had easily obtainable quantities of iron ore and

King Henry gave the abbey to his Master of the Horse, Sir Anthony Browne, who converted the abbot's dwelling into a country mansion. Many abbey buildings, including the church, were demolished around this time.

The deposed monks are said to have laid a curse on the Brownes, saying they would perish by fire or water, a curse which would appear to have come true on more than one occasion, albeit over 250 years later, when several tragedies befell the family. In 1931 a serious fire damaged the west range of Battle Abbey, and restoration work was carried out by the architect Sir Harold Brakspear. The curse was exorcised in 1933!

Battle Abbey estate remained in private hands until 1976, when it was purchased for the nation by the Department of the Environment with aid from American donations. It is now in the care of English Heritage and the surviving ruins and battlefield can be visited. The main building is used as a school and is not open to the public, but during the school summer holidays the former abbot's hall can be viewed.

The ancient battlefield lies to the south of the abbey ruins and stretches eastwards across open countryside.

After landing his forces at Pevensey, William ravaged the southern coastal towns to draw Harold into battle. Harold, who was fighting in the north marched his army south and on the morning of October 14th 1066 the two armies faced each other. The Saxons took up positions at Senlac Ridge, where the abbey ruins now stand and the Normans grouped at nearby Telham, now a hamlet on the Hastings to Battle road. Both armies had approximately 7,000 men and at about 9am the Normans attacked but were repelled. The battle continued into the afternoon with the Normans unable to break the Saxon grip. Part of the Norman army fled, whether in panic or as a strategic move, is not sure and sections of the Saxon army, believing they had triumphed, pursued them onto the lower slopes. William rallied his forces, sent in his cavalry to slaughter this chasing group and then made a determined onslaught against the weakened Saxon position. During the ensuing struggle, Harold was killed.

The remnants of the Saxon army fled northwards, pursued by the Norman cavalry. A last desperate action was fought but by evening all Saxon resistance was gone. The Battle of Hastings was won and lost, signalling the birth of the English nation and the best known date in history.

A diversion from '1066 and all that', which illustrates the British love of animals, can be found in the abbey grounds in the form of the gravestone of a family pet. The dog, which died in 1881, a 'faithful and loving friend', belonged to past owners of the abbey estate. However, there was still some concession to the events of 1066; his name was Norman!

The imposing 14th century abbey gatehouse which dominates the centre of Battle was built in 1338 as fortification against possible French invasion. Standing beside the gates is the Pilgrims Rest. It was erected around 1420 on the site of a 12th century building and was the guest quarters for pilgrims visiting the abbey. It is now a restaurant. The area in front of the abbey gates is known as the Abbey Green. Here can be seen a bullring, used for the once popular pastime of bull-baiting. Battle was a centre for a thriving gunpowder industry in the 17th century and it is on Abbey Green that the effigy of Guy Fawkes, the perpetrator of the greatest gunpowder plot, is burned at the renowned Battel Bonfire Boyes Bonfire Night celebrations each year. Marbles matches are also played there every Good Friday morning.

On the opposite side of High Street to the abbey is Langton Hall, which is used for functions as well as housing the town's museum. It was formerly the home of Elizabeth Langton who was instrumental in setting up the town's first school, when she left money in her will for the purpose.

A popular attraction can be found nearby at Yesterday's World, where exhibits are displayed in individual shops of the Victorian and Edwardian period.

Close by is the parish church of St Mary the Virgin, founded in 1115 by Abbot Ralph for the people of 'Battel', which had by this time become a village which had grown up around the monastery. The only remaining part of the original church is the square Norman font. From the middle of the 12th century the monks began to enlarge the church and the tower was erected in 1440. The north aisle was also added in the 15th century.

Among the many points of interest in this beautiful church are impressive wall paintings and brasses and the tomb of Sir Anthony Browne and his wife Alice. A modern stained glass window, commemorating the English and Norman armies was installed in 1984 and designed by Michael Farrah Bell.

In the south aisle is the burial place of the last abbot of Battle Abbey, John Hammond. After the dissolution of the monasteries, Abbot Hammond was provided with a pension of £100 a year and moved to a house just to the east of the church, where he died in 1546. The building has now been converted to two dwellings.

In the churchyard of St Mary's is the tomb of Isaac Ingalls who, according to his tombstone, was 120 years old when he died in 1796. The Deanery, which stands behind the church, dates from the Elizabethan period.

Among other interesting buildings in the eastern end of the town is The Chequers Inn which dates from the 16th century. Opposite is the area of land known as Lake Meadow, owned by the National Trust. The views from this point are impressive across to Caldbec Hill and the old windmill.

Also to the east is the busy Battle railway station and for those interested in architecture, it is well worth a visit, for there are surely not many more picturesque stations in the country. It was opened in 1852 and designed by William Tress to harmonize with the town.

Returning to the High Street, there are many interesting buildings to be found in this bustling thoroughfare. One hotel was built in 1688 from stone from the abbey after the dissolution of the monasteries and the impressive frontage of Priory House dates from the 18th century. The Old Pharmacy is 15th century and once sold musical instruments.

Any new development in Battle is designed to fit in with its older surroundings and the tasteful Abbey Court shopping area is no exception.

An inn has stood on the site of the George Hotel for over 600 years. The present building is 18th century and once served as the town hall and courthouse. The military was stationed there during the Napoleonic Wars.

Mount Street, at the top end of the High Street, has many interesting buildings and was once the main London road until the A2100 was built. The building now occupied by Friday-Ad was once the local blacksmith's shop and is adjoined by several picturesque 17th and 18th century weatherboarded properties. The crooked Lewinscroft, a former coaching inn, the first part of which was built in the 15th century, is now converted to six dwellings, bearing the names of Saxon knights who fell at the Battle of Hastings. The building has served several purposes and was once a hospital and army barracks.

The well-preserved windmill dominates the skyline and is built on a site believed to have been a Saxon observation post at the Battle of Hastings. The cosy Kings Head pub and the Roman Catholic and Baptist churches are also in Mount Street.

Back in the High Street, opposite Mount Street, a plaque on the building now occupied by a building society explains that it was once the medieval Guildhall. It is believed an underground tunnel once connected the building to Battle Abbey. Close by is The Almonry, dating from the 15th century. It once formed part of the commercial centre of the town. In Western Avenue is a pretty row of timbered cottages and an unusual memorial can be seen at the zebra crossing in High Street, where a stone in the pavement commemorates Ernie Beaney, the man responsible for getting the crossing installed.

Out of the town along the North Trade Road is Battle Hospital. This was formerly the workhouse and known as The Stone House.

Mount Street

Crowhurst

Situated south of Battle and just three miles north-west of Hastings, the village of Crowhurst has, in recent years, become more and more a suburb of that town as new development creeps ever closer. However, it still manages to retain its individuality and community spirit and is a pleasant place to visit. The many footpaths in the area, provide the walker with a great variety of scenery and there are many surviving old houses, some dating from the 14th century. The village is served by a railway station on the Hastings to Charing Cross line, village shops and two public houses, The Plough and The Inn at Crowhurst.

The first mention of Crowhurst was in 771, when a Charter of King Offa of Mercia, gave 8 hides in Croghyrst, to the Bishop of Selsey and a church was built. In the reign of Edward the Confessor the manor was owned by Earl Harold, (later King Harold), and after the Norman Conquest by Walter Fitz Lambert, whose family held it for 200 years. The manor of Crowhurst suffered badly at the hands of the Normans and in the Domesday Book, Croherste is decribed as 'devastated'.

On the south side of the church stand the ruins of the old Manor House, built in the late 12th century by Walter de Scotney, who accompanied King Richard I on his third crusade and was chief steward to the Earl of Gloucester. De Scotney was later charged with attempting to poison the Earl and his brother. He was found guilty at Winchester and executed in 1259. The Earl, despite losing his hair, survived the murder attempt, but his brother died. The manor was then taken over by the Crown and was granted by Henry III to Peter of Savoy.

For nearly 200 years the kings of England were patrons of the church, until in 1412 the Manor of Crowhurst was granted to Sir John Pelham by Henry IV and the present parish church was erected and dedicated to St George.

Its best known feature is the giant yew tree, which is claimed to be a thousand years old. The trunk, held together by iron bands, is over 40 feet in circumference. The surrounding iron railings were erected in 1907 to

Crowhurst Church and its ancient yew tree

save it from further damage. The tree is so cracked that a grown man can stand inside. It is said that the Normans once hanged a Saxon soldier from the tree when he refused to divulge the whereabouts of Harold's treasure.

Inside the church, which has seen much rebuilding through the years, are memorials to the Papillon family, who inherited the Manor of Crowhurst in 1838 and were great benefactors to the church. The father of Mrs Papillon, the Rev Thomas Garnier, Dean of Lincoln, took part in the first Boat Race in 1829, rowing for Oxford.

The Rev J P Bacon-Phillips, rector between 1889-1917, was an eccentric character who gained a reputation for letter-writing to national and local newspapers. He was a champion of the homeless and is said to have written thousands of letters on this and many other subjects during and after his time at Crowhurst. There are memorial windows to his wife and daughter within the church.

The village school, which stands opposite the church, was opened in 1843, when Squire Thomas Papillon gave land and a donation for it to be built. It was modernised and enlarged in 1958.

The disused Crowhurst quarry has for many years been a haven for wildlife and also supports a wide variety of fauna. One of the largest badger setts in the country is established there. Unfortunately, many badgers perished while trying to cross the newly electrified railway line some years ago, but British Rail have since made great efforts to provide safe pathways for the creatures to follow.

Until 1969 a giant viaduct stood on the nearby Crowhurst marshes, which carried the railway line from Bexhill. It was built in 1902 as part of the four mile stretch of line linking Bexhill with the main Hastings to Charing Cross line at Crowhurst. The line was closed in 1964 and the viaduct spectacularly demolished in 1969. Fragments can still be seen today.

Timber from the woods surrounding Crowhurst was used to repair the fortifications at Rye in 1385, when over 200 oak trees were felled for the purpose.

Catsfield

The village of Catsfield is set amid rolling hills and woodland, south-west of Battle.

It is not certain how the village got its name, but one theory is that it was derived from the Saxon tribe of Catti, who were early settlers in the area. Before the Norman Conquest, the manor was owned by the Saxon, Elfalm and was among the first places to be sacked by the invading Normans. After the Conquest, the manor passed to a Norman priest named Wrenc and in the Domesday Book the area is shown as Cedesfille.

Catsfield today has a profusion of charming old cottages along its main street and a delightful 'olde worlde' pub, The White Hart. The steepled Methodist church stands close to the centre of the village and the ancient parish church of St Laurence, with its square tower and shingled spire stands in picturesque surroundings a quarter of a mile away.

Buried in the graveyard of this beautiful Norman church is Thomas Brassey, the famous railway engineer, who with his partner George Stephenson, laid railways across five continents. Brassey, who died in 1870, aged 65, was the son of a farmer and began his railway construction work with the Grand Junction in England and eventually opened up the expanses of India, Canada and Australia.

The memorial to Lady Brassey

His son, Lord Thomas Brassey, became the Liberal Member of Parliament for Hastings in 1868 and Lady Brassey gained fame as an authoress and collector. Her books described her worldwide yachting voyages. She died tragically at sea and a memorial to her can be seen in the church and many of her collected pieces can be seen in Hastings Museum. There is also reference in the church to Normanhurst House (now demolished), which was once the seat of the Brassey family.

The memorial over the tower arch to John Fuller is by the sculptor Nollekens. Fuller was the uncle of Mad Jack Fuller *(see Brightling),* who during his life suffered from temporary blindness. In gratitude for his recovery he founded a charity, money from which was to be distributed to six local blind people. The charity is still in existence today and is administered by the East Sussex Association for the Blind.

The oak tree which stands close to the churchyard gate was planted in 1966 to mark the 900th anniversary of the Battle of Hastings. It replaced another oak which had stood there since Norman times and is today remembered on the village sign.

During the Second World War a bomb disposal unit was stationed in Catsfield. A sad reminder of the dangers involved in such work can be found in the graveyard, where two Royal Engineers, Lieut Cunningham and Sergeant Mack are buried. Both lost their lives while attempting to disarm an unexploded bomb which fell close to the village in 1944.

In 1791, Marie Antoinette, the doomed French queen, sent her closest friend, Princess de Lamballe, to Catsfield to deposit several of her jewels with Lady Gibbs of Catsfield Place for safe-keeping. Within a year of her return to France, the princess was executed.

Mountfield

It was once thought that the area around Mountfield, to the north of Battle, had large unexploited seams of coal and in 1876 a 2000 feet deep exploratory bore hole was drilled.

However, the search proved fruitless, but a substance was found which has provided the area with a thriving industry ever since. Gypsum is a sulphate of calcium, used today in the manufacture of plasterboards and cement, and the gypsum mine at Mountfield is among the few still working in the country.

The actual entrance is tucked away in Limekiln Woods and the catacomb workings spread for miles under the countryside. There is a second smaller mine four miles away at Brightling and the only obvious sign of industry is the aerial cableway which connects the two places.

Mountfield is linked to the surrounding villages of Netherfield and Brightling by winding roads running through some of the most unspoilt countryside in Sussex. Don't worry if the roads become a little narrow, or a blade or two of grass appears in the centre; persevere, they all reach their destinations!

The Norman parish church of All Saints, with its magnificent porch and rare wall paintings, is beautifully positioned and well worth a visit.

Netherfield

Netherfield, situated off the B2096 between Battle and Brightling, stands on a high point overlooking beautiful Forestry Commission land.

The parish church was a gift to the village by Lady Webster in memory of her husband, Sir Godfrey Webster of Battle Abbey. It was dedicated in 1860. Prior to this, services were held in the barn of a local farm.

The rather austere design was by S S Teulon, the controversial Victorian architect, who also designed Holy Trinity Church in Hastings. The cavernous interior contains many unusual features.

The church is dedicated to St John the Baptist, a fact rather grotesquely commemorated by the painting on the north wall, showing the unfortunate St John's head on a platter carried by Salome. It was painted by the 17th century artist Giovanni Barbieri, who used himself as the model for the features.

The schoolhouse which adjoins the churchyard was also given by Lady Webster in 1859. It closed as a school in 1961.

Netherfield Hall, opposite the church, provides a convenient stop for coffee. Nearby Netherfield Place is now a high-quality restaurant and the village is served by two public houses, the White Hart and The Netherfield Arms.

Courtesy of Parochial Church Council, St John the Baptist, Netherfield

Brightling

Brightling is situated five miles from Battle and a visit is rewarded with spectacular views in all directions across the unspoilt countryside, many fine walks and a marvellous air of tranquillity.

The village featured prominently in BBC television's 1995 production of 'Cold Comfort Farm'.

But undoubtedly the most famous attraction of this delightful place are the folly buildings of John 'Mad Jack' Fuller, the wealthy, larger-than-life squire of Brightling and MP for East Sussex in the 19th century.

These architectural oddities of a bygone romantic age, scattered around the village and surrounding fields, are one of the best preserved groups of follies in Britain and lasting reminders of Brightling's most celebrated resident.

Fuller was also a great champion of the arts and sciences, a patron of the artist J M Turner, who painted views of Brightling, and a founder member of the Royal Institution of Great Britain. The Observatory, high on Brightling Down, was built by Fuller in 1818 and once contained the most advanced equipment of the time. It is now a private home.

But perhaps the most unusual sight is the pyramid in the churchyard of St Thomas a Beckett, where John Fuller was laid to rest in 1834. He was said to have been interred dressed in full evening dress, sitting at a table with a meal before him. This, of course, was not true and he is buried in the conventional way beneath the floor of the pyramid. But everyone loves a good story and this is typical of the tales, usually made up by the locals, which surround many of Fuller's follies.

Inside the ancient church there are many interesting features. The church was Fuller's pride and joy and he made many donations, among them the unique barrel organ and a peal of bells. A memorial bust of the great man gazes down from the wall.

The pyramid tomb of John Fuller

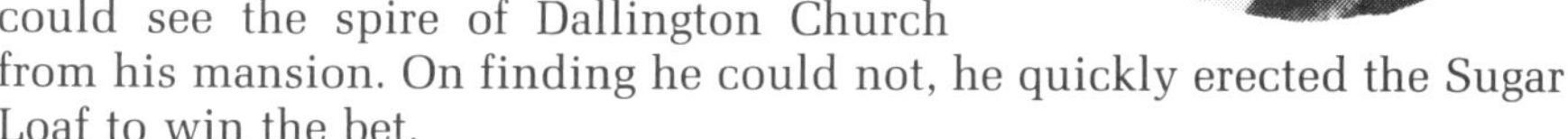

The Brightling Needle, built by Fuller circa 1810, stands on the second highest point in Sussex and the Sugar Loaf, a conical structure at Woods Corner, provides a link with the nearby village of Dallington. The Sugar Loaf was erected as the result of a wager made by Fuller while in London, when he declared he could see the spire of Dallington Church from his mansion. On finding he could not, he quickly erected the Sugar Loaf to win the bet.

Brightling's popular pub, Jack Fuller's, stands half a mile from the centre of the village on the road to Robertsbridge. The building, a converted barn, was once owned by John Fuller. Now bearing all the trappings of a cosy English country pub, it is renowned for its fine food.

The area is also known for its gypsum mine *(see Mountfield)*. The transportation system is carefully disguised to fit unobtrusively into the landscape as it carries the raw gypsum to the processing plant at nearby Mountfield.

Whether folly hunting or merely taking in the peaceful 'away from it all' atmosphere, a visit to Brightling can be a rewarding experience.

Away from the village is Socknersh Manor, a fine 17th century half-timbered house, which can be viewed from the footpath which passes its gates.

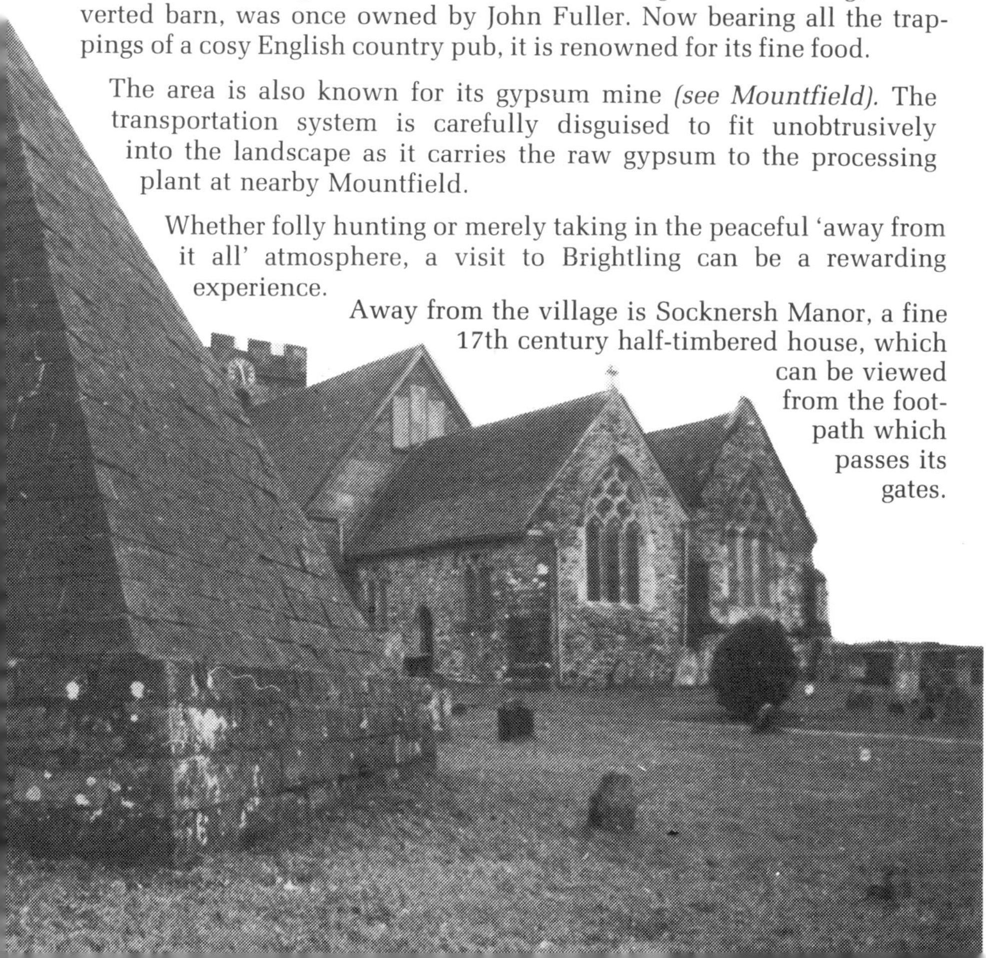

Attached to the outside of the building and supporting the porches at the front and back of the house are pairs of figures known locally as 'the baby eaters'. One pair is gaunt and menacing, the other plump and happy. Why they are called baby-eaters and who they are supposed to depict remains a mystery, but they could have some connection to the strange and macabre legend — peculiar to East Sussex — which accused certain members of influential families of cannibalism in bygone days *(see Brede)*.

It must be stressed they are on private property and to respect the owners' privacy, the house and figures must only be viewed from the distance of the marked footpaths.

Dallington and Rushlake Green

The village of Dallington is reached off the B2096 Battle to Heathfield road. It is a picturesque little place with many attractive older buildings. The interesting parish church is worth a visit, where one can judge John Fuller's accuracy when he built the Sugar Loaf replica of the unusual spire, one of only three stone spires to be found in Sussex.

Nearby Rushlake Green also provides an attractive setting, with its old cottages and the Horse and Groom pub surrounding the village green. Warbleton Priory, the surviving part of which is now a private residence and not open to the public, was once occupied by Augustinian monks who moved from Hastings during the reign of Henry IV. Two human skulls, said to belong to 15th century monks at the Priory, have provided the area with a good ghost story over the years. When anyone tried to bury them, the skulls would 'scream' and the person attempting the deed would suffer ill fortune. Earlier this century, one of the skulls came into the possession of the landlord of the Horse and Groom, who thought it would be an attraction for his customers. His beer turned sour!

An unusual memorial can be found in the parish of Dallington, between Woods Corner and Bodle Street. At the side of the road a cross commemorates World War II airman, Peter Crofts (one of The Few), who died when his plane crashed nearby in 1940. The cross was erected on a small plot of land purchased by his mother and is maintained today by the RAF Association. A remembrance service is held there each year.

Also on the road to Bodle Street is the impressive 16th century Redpale Farmhouse, once the home of one of Henry VIII's tutors.

Note the Victorian postbox outside.

The Peter Crotts memorial

In Penehest, which Osborn holds of the Earl of Eu, the abbot has half a hide and there are two villeins with two ploughs and one acre of meadow and wood for two hogs. It is worth fifteen shillings *Domesday Book, 1086*

Penhurst and Ashburnham

Situated in the thinly populated area on the surrounds of Ashburnham Park and sandwiched between the B2096 and B2204 roads, lies Penhurst, the smallest and most obscure place mentioned in this booklet.

The narrow winding lanes leading there will lead you away from the hustle and bustle of the 20th century and transport you back in time. Penhurst consists of a church, a manor house, and a few farm buildings and has changed little since the 16th century. Its dramatic simplicity is a rewarding experience.

Penhurst — where time has stood still

The unique picturesque group of buildings is described as 'a rare and exquisite manorial group'. The Elizabethan manor house is built on the site of an even earlier dwelling and the sandstone church dates from the 14th century. Inside the church is a small 17th century chapel and a Tudor carved oak pulpit. The oak pews were made by local carpenters in 1858 from trees on the nearby Ashburnham estate and there is evidence of a medieval wall painting at the east end of the nave.

The tranquil graveyard contains many fine headstones and is the last resting place of actor Harry H Corbett, famous for his role as Harold in Steptoe and Son, who lived at Ashburnham until 1982.

The ornate copper lamp (a seemingly modern item in a place such as Penhurst), which stands at the church gate, once lit a street in the London Borough of Clerkenwell.

The church has an unusual way of providing heat for the congregation in winter. Although electric heating has now been installed, it is supplemented in severe weather by hot air blown in by an agricultural corn drier.

The rectory once stood to the north west of the church, but has now fallen into ruin since the manor of Penhurst was joined with the vicarage of Ashburnham in 1811. Penhurst was owned by the Ashburnham family from the reign of George III till the 1950s.

The area was once a thriving centre of the Sussex iron industry and in the Elizabethan manor house, built by William Relph, are the last firebacks cast at the Ashburnham Furnace. The picturesque manor house has delightful gardens, a duck pond adjoins the road and the whole group of buildings provides an idyllic scene. Just reflect awhile and drink in the peace.

The village of Ashburnham is reached from Penhurst by the road built by Lord Ashburnham in 1886 for his tenants' use and to enable the parishioners of Ashburnham to convey their dead to Penhurst for burial after the closure of their own churchyard. The road passes the old forge about half-a-mile to the west of the church and a further half-a-mile north, on a bumpy track are the ruins, from around 1820, of the iron furnace, the last to be worked in Sussex. The kiln and outbuildings of a brickworks, near Ponts Green, are yet more pointers to the area's industrial past. The kiln was the last wood-fired type to be used in Sussex and continued working until 1968.

The village of Ashburnham is spread over a wide area, hidden among the maze of lanes. The 'olde worlde' Ash Tree Inn is reached by following the signs to Brownbread Street, and offers fine food and a warm welcome.

The most important and influential family in the village is the one from which it takes its name. The family connection dates to the 12th century and continued unbroken until Lady Catherine Ashburnham died in 1953.

The parish church is reached by entering the grounds of Ashburnham Place from the B2204 and is situated beside the family mansion, which is now occupied by the Ashburnham Christian Trust as a training and conference centre for lay preachers. The gardens in the magnificent Ashburnham Park were laid out by Capability Brown in the 18th century.

The church contains two spectacular monuments to the Ashburnham family, one to John Ashburnham in the Jacobean style and one in baroque style to William.

It is said that the clothes worn by King Charles I at his execution were once kept in the church along with the sheet which was thrown over his body, and a lock of his hair. Strangely for such gruesome items, they were said to have healing qualities if touched.

Ninfield

The village stocks

Ninfield is situated to the west of Bexhill on the A269 and it was at Standard Hill, legend says William the Conqueror raised his colours after the Battle of Hastings. The village sign on the green gives credence to the story by depicting a Norman warrior on horseback. On the site of Standard Hill today is a 17th century house with unusual religious texts engraved into the wall.

Next to the village green, at the entrance to the lane leading to the parish church of St Mary the Virgin, are Ninfield's proudest possessions, the village stocks and whipping post. They are well preserved because they are made of Sussex iron instead of wood. Manchester House, now the village shop, was once a depot for cotton goods from Manchester, which were stored there before being distributed along the south coast.

Hooe

South of Ninfield on the B2095 is the village of Hooe, one of the most peaceful places in the county.

In the 18th century the countryside surrounding the village was even more wild and open than it is today and was a perfect setting for smugglers. The Red Lion pub was once the haunt of a notorious group known as the Groombridge Gang — the landlord himself even being a member.

The parish church is a delight. It is situated away from the village and lies secluded at the end of a long and very narrow lane. There is much of interest inside the church and the views from the churchyard across the Pevensey Levels are beautiful.

Wartling

The tiny village of Wartling is situated off the A259 and sits on a bend in the road to Herstmonceux. There are several old cottages grouped around the parish church and Lamb Inn.

The heron has taken a liking to this quiet spot and has become the symbolic bird of the village. It has nested there for over a hundred years and today there are two heronries close to the church.

It is fitting that inside the 13th century parish church of St Mary Magdalene one of the finest features is the lectern, in the shape of a heron. It is a magnificent piece of craftsmanship and was carved in elm from the Glyndebourne estate by Martin Wynn Pierce. It was commissioned as a memorial to the Rev Harry Osborn, who died in 1976.

Another outstanding feature can be seen above the chancel arch, where a particularly well restored Royal Coat of Arms, dated 1731, can be illuminated by pressing a button on the wall close to the organ. Note also the attractive box pews.

From the serene churchyard the views stretch to Beachy Head in the west.

Herstmonceux

The village of Herstmonceux is on the A271 and within its large parish are the hamlets of Cowbeech, Flowers Green, Stunts Green, Gingers Green, Windmill Hill and Bodle Street.

Before the Norman Conquest, the name Herst or Hurst, meaning a forest or wood, was taken by a local family living in the area and in 1131 the manor was transferred to a great grandson of William the Conqueror, Drogo de Monceux. His son Ingleram de Monceux married Idonea de Herst and their son was known as Waleran de Herst Monceux. Hence the village name!

It is probable the original village of Herstmonceux consisted of a manor, a church and a few homesteads. The main village street was once a separate hamlet and became the principal thoroughfare in 1766 when the Battle to Lewes road was built.

Today, Herstmonceux has a useful selection of shops, eating places and two public houses in its main street. The Woolpack in the centre of the village was once a coaching inn and The Brewer's Arms is a timber-clad building dating from the 17th century.

Among the older buildings in the village are the 16th century Sundial and 18th century Higham House and Higham Cottage, which formerly served as the workhouse. Herstmonceux once had a lunatic asylum. It was situated at Bedlam Cottage.

Herstmonceux's famous moated castle is no longer open to the public, but the grounds are accessible during summer. From 1946 the castle was the headquarters of the Royal Greenwich Observatory until April 1990, when the operation was moved to Cambridge. On the road to Wartling the domed telescope housings can still be seen. The largest once housed the Sir Isaac Newton telescope, now sited in the Canary Islands.

Herstmonceux Castle was built in 1441 by Sir Roger Fiennes, a veteran of Agincourt and Treasurer to the Household of Henry VI. A present day descendant is Sir Ranulph Fiennes, the Arctic explorer.

It was one of the earliest brick built castles in England, but eventually became a ruin and was demolished in 1777, when much of the material was used to build Herstmonceux Place. In 1910 it was partially restored and in 1936 rebuilt to its former glory by Sir Paul Latham.

The castle was once renowned for its ghosts. It is said a nine-feet-tall drummer walked the battlements at night, and the apparition of a lady regularly climbed the staircase. Both were almost certainly the inventions of smugglers operating in the area and meant to keep the curious away.

Herstmonceux Place was built in 1777 and was originally owned by the Hare-Nayler family and later by Sir Paul Latham, during the restoration of the castle. It has now been converted to flats but is still a listed building.

Off the A271, along the cul-de-sac road leading to the parish church and castle, is the house named Lime Park, site of a former monastery and once known as The Lime. It stands opposite The Welcome Stranger pub and is the former home of Augustus Hare, Victorian author and traveller. In 1957 the stables were converted into a rectory, which was used until 1983 but Lime Park is now divided into four dwellings. It was at Lime Park that an electricity generator was situated in 1909. Herstmonceux was one of the first villages in Sussex to have electricity.

There are many other older houses and cottages in this area. The Welcome Stranger public house is one of the smallest, quaintest inns in Sussex. It's quite an experience taking a drink here, and is more like stepping into someone's living room. It's a pub in the old tradition; no frills, no juke box or one-arm bandits. It is believed the pub's name is derived from the commemoration of the birth of an heir to the Lord of the Manor.

The beautiful parish church of All Saints, mentioned in the Domesday Book, stands about two miles from the village centre and is of Saxon origin. There is little of the original church remaining today, the earliest part dating from 1180. Additions were made in the 13th and 14th centuries, when the south porch was built. The church stands in a delightful position, surrounded by trees and overlooking the Pevensey levels to the sea.

The most spectacular part of the church is the Dacre Chapel which was added around 1450. It was given by the Fiennes family, then occupants of the castle, and is one of the earliest examples of church brickwork in Sussex. The ornate tomb, with its effigies in Milanese armour, was erected in 1534 to the memory of Thomas, 8th Lord Dacre, who died in 1533 and his son, Sir Thomas Fiennes, in 1528. In 1970 the tomb was extensively restored by local mason George Elliott.

All church towers in Sussex seem to have some unique feature. The tower of All Saints is the only one in the county which forms part of the west end of the nave. The tower is built of sandstone with a timber spire.

An interesting American connection is found in the Monceux McCants memorial window. The family is a survival of the Monceux descent which continued in America for many generations. In the churchyard is the grave of author Augustus Hare, who died in 1903.

Herstmonceux once boasted a sweet-making factory and a brewery, both now gone, but one industry which has survived for 160 years is trug making. The Sussex Trug is an all-purpose basket which was first produced in the village by Thomas Smith, who exhibited the product at the Great Exhibition of 1851.

The unique churchyard at the nearby picturesque village of Hellingly is well worth a visit. The form of circular burial ground (ciric) is the only one of its kind in Sussex to remain intact. The circle was the pagan symbol of immortality and the method of burial was to lay the dead in raised mounds. The churchyard is surrounded by a charming collection of old cottages

A Sussex trug

Pevensey

Courtesy of Priory Court Hotel

Standing on the A259 west of Bexhill is Pevensey, one of the most historic places in England. The site of the castle dates back almost 2000 years.

It was at Pevensey that William I landed his invading army in 700 boats in 1066, but nearly 800 years earlier it was the site of the Roman stronghold of Anderida, one of a series of fortresses placed along the southern shore.

Today the village of Pevensey lies over a mile inland from the sea but the original Anderida was built on a small island. The name Pevensey dates from AD792 and means 'the island of Pefe'. The sea reached the outer walls of the castle until the 13th century and the harbour was navigable until 1700.

The outer walls are the remains of the earliest building and are considered to be the finest example of Roman building in the country. They are 12 feet thick and between 25 and 30 feet high, enclosing an area of 10 acres and were built between 250 and 300AD.

After the departure of the Romans, the fortress was occupied in AD491 by Aella the Saxon and little is known of its history until Earl Godwin raided it in 1042 and 1049.

After the Battle of Hastings and the defeat of King Harold, William I retained the six administrative areas of Sussex used by the Saxons. These were known as Rapes and William ordered each to be protected by a castle. Pevensey came into the possession of William's half-brother, Robert, Earl of Mortain, who soon began to build a fortress within the Roman walls. The ruins of this pentagonal keep, which had five towers and a moat, covers one and a half acres and can been seen in the south-east corner. The gate-house, walls and towers of the inner courtyard, were added in the 13th century.

Pevensey became part of the Cinque Ports as a 'limb' of Hastings and despite the problems caused by the gradual silting of the harbour, continued for many years to supply its quota of ships to the King's navy. Pevensey was considered important enough to have its own mint. Coins were made there from 1076.

The castle has had a violent history. In the years following the Conquest, it was besieged by King Willam Rufus, King Stephen and Simon de Montfort and in 1399 was gallantly defended by Lady Pelham against the Yorkists.

Twice it narrowly escaped demolition. Elizabeth I's order for the castle to be dismantled was surprisingly ignored and during the Cromwellian period, the castle was sold to a builder for demolition. Thankfully he didn't complete the task and after the Restoration it became crown property.

By the time of William III in the 17th century, the castle was granted to the Duke of Portland and in the 18th century was in the hands of Spencer Compton, Earl of Wilmington, later Viscount Pevensey. It descended by marriage to the Duke of Devonshire, who presented it to the nation. The ruins are now in the care of English Heritage.

During the Second World War, when the country was threatened by German invasion, the castle was once more prepared for action, when the towers were reinforced and carefully disguised pill boxes were added.

Although most people visit Pevensey to view the castle, there are many other interesting features in the village. Opposite the castle gate is the old Mint House, which dates from 1342 and was built on the site of the Norman mint.

Further along the main street is the Court House. It was once the town hall and is claimed to be the smallest in England. Despite its size, Pevensey retained its mayor and corporation until 1883. The upper storey was used as the court room and the ground floor was the village lock-up with two cells. The Court House now houses a museum.

The happy-go-lucky friar, scholar and writer, Andrew Borde, the original 'Merry Andrew', who served as physician to King Henry VIII, once lived in Pevensey. Among his best-known writings is 'Merry Tales of the Mad Men of Gotham'.

Pevensey Church is dedicated to St Nicholas and was started in the reign of King John in the 13th century. Its main features are the long chancel and ornate memorial to John Wheatley, a wealthy parishioner in Elizabethan times. The windows in the south wall of the chancel date to 1215.

There are several excellent pubs and eating houses in Pevensey. The Smugglers Inn, as its name implies, was a favourite haunt for 'the gentlemen' and the landlord can tell you a pretty convincing ghost story. During its history it has been used as a courtroom and a previous landlady supplemented her income by making rope for the village fishermen.

The Priory Court Hotel was built in the 15th century. Some of the material used came from Pevensey Castle. It was once the vicarage, but was converted to a hotel and restaurant 50 years ago. The village's other popular public house, The Royal Oak and Castle, stands opposite the castle gates.

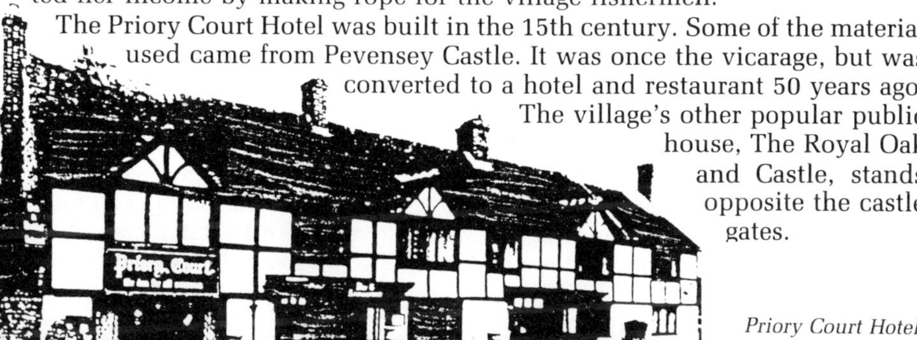

Priory Court Hotel

To the south of Pevensey is the popular small holiday resort of Pevensey Bay. There are some fine examples of Martello Towers along the shore line and one has been converted to a dwelling house.

To the east is Norman's Bay, formerly known as Pevensey Sluice, also a popular place for holidaymakers. The narrow B2182 road which leads eastwards to Cooden and Bexhill, passes the ancient Star Inn, yet another historic pub with smuggling connections.

The area is served by British Rail's coastway line with stations at Norman's Bay, Pevensey Bay and Pevensey and Westham. One of the best views of the castle can be seen from the train.

Westham

Westham is less than a mile to the west of Pevensey and stands within the shadows of the castle wall, but is keen to keep its own identity. Any previous suggestions to link it with its neighbour have been vigorously resisted. However, this fierce pride in identity doesn't seem to have influenced the local pub. It's named The Pevensey Castle!

There are several picturesque old cottages and houses in the main street, but the village's main attraction is its church, the first to be built by the Normans after the Conquest. This church set the pattern for Norman church-building; the tearing down of Saxon masonry and the building up of churches in their own style, or the erecting of new churches where none existed. The massive tower was added in the 13th century. The interior is notable for its Norman arch in the south transept and the beautiful 15th century carved oak screen.

An unusual item in the church is a fragment of King Solomon's temple, brought to the church by a former vicar, the Rev Howard Hopley. In 1860, while helping on the excavation work in Jerusalem he decided to bring back a piece of the temple as a souvenir and seemingly unbecoming of a vicar, he chipped a piece off!

The church has had some colourful vicars during its history, among them Brian Duppa, in 1625, who was tutor to Charles II and had spent much time with the doomed Charles I during his imprisonment. It would appear that Charles II had not always followed the spiritual guidance laid before him and when the cleric was at death's door, the king knelt beside his bed and begged forgiveness.

William Leeke, curate from 1829, was a standard bearer at the Battle of Waterloo and held services for coastguards serving in the nearby Martello Towers. The services were held at irregular hours to confuse smugglers.

In the graveyard of the church, the 'plague stones' in the shape of a cross, mark the communal grave of victims of the Black Death in 1666.

The picturesque cannon on the village green dates from the 19th century.

To the north

Sedlescombe

After leaving Hastings to the north, the A21 soon passes Norton's Farm, where a museum and farm trail are open during the season. After five miles the road forks right to the beautiful village of Sedlescombe. With its picturesque 15th, 16th and 17th century half-timbered houses surrounding the sloping village green, it is rightly considered one of the prettiest places in the south-east.

The name is derived from Saxon times. 'Combe' meaning valley and 'setle' residence. The village is mentioned in the Domesday Book, and a church 'ecclesiola' is also recorded.

The Battle of Hastings took place three miles from Sedlescombe and the village suffered badly at the hands of the marauding Normans. After the Conquest many landowners were forced to pay rents to Battle Abbey.

In 1876 an iron pot was found at Sedlescombe, containing 3,000 coins of the realm of King Edward the Confessor (1042-1066), thought to have been the treasure of King Harold, and hidden during the Battle of Hastings. Some of these coins can be seen in Hastings Museum.

It seems hard to believe that the tranquil village of Sedlescombe we see today was once part of a great industrial area during the 17th century, when it was an important cog in the Sussex iron industry. Iron has been made in Sedlescombe since Roman times, and the road which runs through the village follows the line of the original Roman road, built to link various iron-workings in Sussex to London.

Today the village has a wide variety of local businesses and shops and is a popular venue for diners.

On the right before entering the village is the entrance to the famous Pestalozzi Children's Village, founded in 1959 on the site of Oaklands, the former home of popular village squire and painter, Hercules Brabazon (his initials can be seen on Tanyard Cottage and other buildings in the village).

The Pestalozzi Village is home to over 100 children from the poorer areas of Nepal, Thailand, Zambia, Jordan, India and Tibet, who come to England to gain academic and practical skills, and eventually return to their homelands to pass on their acquired knowledge to their less privileged countrymen. The village is run on the ideals of Swiss educationalist Johann Heinrich Pestalozzi, who died in 1827, and who during his lifetime set up several orphanages for children of different nationalities in rural surroundings.

The bridge crossing the River Brede was built in the 18th century by local builder, John Catt, whose name can be seen on the structure. The river, now no more than a stream, was in ancient times a tidal arm of the sea. It was once a quarter-of-a-mile wide and filled the valley as it flowed down to the sea at Rye, some 15 miles away. The Saxons named the river Brede, which means broad. It was once the only means of communication and Sedlescombe was for hundreds of years a river port.

The Tithe Barn once housed a permanent exhibition of paintings by Hercules Brabazon, whose work is still in demand today.

At the rear of the Bridge Garage there once stood a water mill, which ground corn until 1750, when it was utilised to make gunpowder. Sedlescombe gunpowder was said to be the best in Europe. Barrack Cottage, on the opposite side of the main street, was the home of the guardian of the gunpowder and the finished product was stored on a farm a mile away from the village, to await transportation. The industry was not without risk and in December 1764, 'before breakfast', it is told, four men died following an explosion in the sifting house.

On the wall of the Bridge Garage, once a forge, can be seen a reminder of the days of iron in a fireback dated 1649, which depicts Richard Lennard, the craftsman who designed them. Another Sedlescombe fireback can be seen at Hastings Museum.

One local industry which has survived for over 500 years in nearby Petley Wood, is charcoal burning. There is still a demand for charcoal and the production methods used today are the same as in the days when Battle Abbey was a customer in the 15th century. This is the last remaining site in

The Sedlescombe fireback

England which produces charcoal on such a scale by traditional methods.

Another unusual but much-used facility in Sedlescombe is the Pets Cemetery, containing many memorials and tributes to favourite pets. It is situated in woodland in Hurst Lane. Viewing is by appointment only.

The well on the village green was dug in 1900, and the pump and shelter were erected by the Rev John Pratt, in memory of his three daughters. Mains water was not supplied to Sedlescombe until 1960.

Holmes House, now a popular eating house, was a butcher's shop for 150 years and bears the name of the last butcher to ply his trade there.

The ancient Queen's Head pub stands invitingly at the corner of the village green and opposite is the hotel named Brickwall, once the home of the ironmasters named Farnden in the 17th century. The Old Manor House, a fine timbered building, dates from 1611.

The parish church of St John the Baptist stands half-a-mile from the village green. It is positioned in the centre of the ancient parish so ensuring that in days gone by no one would have to walk more than two miles to reach it.

It is believed a church has stood on the hill-top site since Saxon times, though no traces of the original building can be seen today.

The present church is built from Sussex ironstone and dates from the 13th century. It was enlarged in the 15th century and restoration took place in 1838 and 1874. The tower contains six bells and all were, quite uniquely, cast at the same foundry in Whitechapel between 1595 and 1929.

An unusual possession of the church is the seating plan of 1632, a tracing of which hangs in the south porch. It shows the names of the parishioners, the seat allotted to them, and the house where they lived. At this time the law stated that attendance at church on Sundays was compulsory and the churchwarden visited absentees to enquire of their non-attendance and if found lacking in genuine excuse, were given a severe reprimand and fined a shilling. Many of the houses on the plan are still in existence today.

Other interesting features include the 16th century font and oak cover and a model of the church made from gypsum by John Catt.

Among the many fine memorials in the church are those of the Brabazon family and iron memorials to the Bishop family inset into the north aisle. Only ironmasters were allowed to be commemorated by these iron slabs.

Whatlington

Whatlington, meaning 'wheat-field settlement', is situated on the A21 about six miles north-west of Hastings. There are many attractive cottages and impressive thatched dwellings, a picturesque converted chapel and the fine old Royal Oak Inn, which sits on a triangular plot close to the village green.

In ancient times Whatlington's most famous Lord of the Manor was none other than King Harold himself, until 1066 when . . . well you know the rest!

The beautiful little Norman church is signposted on the road to Battle. It is situated in a secluded position with fine views. An ancient yew tree, said to be around a thousand years old, stands in the churchyard.

Much of the original Norman work remains, including the nave which retains its ancient roof. The east window dates from 1275.

For such a small church there are some outstanding features. Perhaps the most impressive is the 19th century French carved pulpit, with three angels at the base. The lectern, in the shape of an eagle, is by the same craftsman. Both items were displayed at the Great Exhibition in 1851.

The entrance to the church is through the bell tower and the ropes hang down in front of the door. I am assured the resulting congestion when worshippers arrive for services causes no real problem!

The A21 continues to Robertsbridge and passes the hamlet of John's Cross and its historic inn.

Robertsbridge and Salehurst

It seems hard to imagine now that the main A21 Hastings to London road once bisected the quiet picturesque village of Robertsbridge and that giant lorries nearly touched the buildings as they trundled their way through. Since the opening of the bypass in 1989, local folk — and visitors — have been able to enjoy long-awaited peace.

The ancient village has a fine selection of older buildings, some of them dating to Tudor times. There is also a haunted inn and Robertsbridge is the home of the cricket bat manufacturers, Gray-Nicholls.

To the east of the village once stood a Cistercian Abbey, founded in 1176 by Robert de St Martin, who originated from Normandy. Robert de St Martin is believed to have built a bridge across the Rother, and it is said this is how the village got its name. The abbey seal depicted a bridge with a river beneath and church above. Little remains of the abbey today except a few remnants of the refectory wall at Abbey Farm, now a private residence.

At the entrance to the village is the George public house, mentioned by the Sussex author Hillaire Beloc in his book, 'The Four Men'. The George was one of Beloc's favourite watering holes (he praised the quality of the port) and was a frequent visitor.

The author and broadcaster Malcolm Muggeridge was a celebrated resident of the village for many years.

The building which is now the Seven Stars Inn was constructed in 1194 and the earliest occupants were the Cistercian monks from the nearby abbey. It became an inn in 1380 during the reign of Richard II and is famous for its ghosts which have featured many times in books on the subject. The ghost of Andrew the monk is said to wander the corridors and a poltergeist throws items around the kitchen. The landlord will gladly enlighten you further.

Gray-Nicholls have been making cricket bats in Robertsbridge for over a hundred years. Established in 1876, the company has supplied many of the great players through the years, including the legendary W G Grace. Bats are made from local willow and the factory is situated on the Robertsbridge to Brightling road.

Further along this road is The Ostrich public house, which stands opposite the railway station. Close by is the Hutterian Society of Brothers, a community of over 200 men, women and children, who live in the former TB. isolation hospital and finance their simple way of life by making wooden play equipment for children. They use no currency, share a common belief and the brotherhood maintains its own school and makes its own clothes on the premises.

On looking round Robertsbridge the visitor will note the absence of a parish church, a strange omission for a village of this size. The reason is that although today Robertsbridge is the main centre of population, the small settlement of Salehurst, half a mile away, was the first hub of the area and still gives its name to the parish today.

Mentioned in the Domesday Book as Salhert, the centre of Salehurst consists of a dozen houses, a public house and the magnificent parish church of Saint Mary the Virgin. Started between 1220 and 1250 the church is reputed to have the longest and highest nave in Sussex of its period. It is built from the variety of stone known as Hastings sandstone, and withstood the elements for over 800 years until restoration was needed following bomb damage inflicted in 1944. The massive tower was erected in two stages and is built within the church. The walls are several feet thick and the whole structure is a remarkable piece of engineering.

There are many items of interest within this historic church, the most revered being the 12th century font, which legend says was given by Richard the Lionheart in gratitude to Abbot William for securing his release from captivity in Bavaria.

The churchyard takes up an area of 1½ acres and contains several interesting tombstones, particularly those decorated with small ornamental plaques of terra cotta, made by Jonathan Harmer of Heathfield, between 1800 and 1839. The architect Sir Edward Lutyens designed the tomb of Lord Milner in the south-east of the churchyard. Lord Milner, a statesman, resided at Wigsell, the large, well-preserved Manor House which still stands in the north-east part of the parish.

By the north door is the grave of Peter Sparke, who died in 1683, allegedly 127 years old.

In 1830 a cottage stood on the front entrance steps to the church. The vicar purchased the cottage, demolished it and had the present access and steps built.

Salehurst also has a connection with the story of Lovers' Seat *(see Fairlight)*, for it was here that Lieutenant Lamb and Elizabeth Boyes lived at the property known as Highams House. Their daughter Elizabeth was born there and baptised in Salehurst parish church in 1789.

In medieval days the main road from London passed the church and it was not until after the Reformation and the closure of the abbey that new roads were built and Robertsbridge became the main centre of population.

Bodiam

Situated in the beautiful unspoilt Rother Valley, Bodiam is reached by following the signs off the A21 at the southern approaches to Hurst Green or by turning off the Sedlescombe to Hawkhurst road.

The outstanding feature of the village is its moated castle. It is the last great medieval military fortress to have been built in England and its picturesque shell is considered to be the finest ruined castle in the country.

The castle was built in the reign of Richard II by Sir Edward Dalyngrigge, between the years 1385 and 1390 as a precaution against French attack, when it was thought necessary to protect a then navigable river. However, these attacks failed to materialise and the castle is surprisingly lacking in history. Only twice did it feature in serious conflict when in 1484 it was captured by Richard III and in 1645 during the Civil War when attacked by the parliamentarian troops of Sir William Waller, which left it partially ruined.

The castle fell further and further into decay until in 1828 the Brightling philanthropist, John Fuller *(see Brightling)* purchased it for a sum of £3000, so saving it from complete demolition by a firm of Hastings builders. He carried out necessary repairs and placed a new set of gates at the entrance.

The castle was later sold to Lord Ashcombe, and in 1917 acquired by Lord Curzon, who continued the restoration and maintenance work necessary to bring the building back to its former glory. On his death in 1925 it was bequeathed to the National Trust, in whose capable hands it remains today.

The six feet thick walls stand 40 feet high, and are strengthened at each corner by a circular tower, 60 feet high and 29 feet in diameter. Square towers are placed between them and on the northern side the double tower forms a massive gatehouse. The water-lilied moat is filled directly from the River Rother and today the castle is approached by the causeway on the northern side. In 1970 the moat was dredged to its original depth. There are plenty of places to picnic around the castle grounds and ample parking space is available. The area is well suited for walking the banks of the River Rother. There is also an excellent tea shop adjacent to the castle grounds.

Bodiam Castle has a fairybook ambience and it seems easy to visualise the knights of old, in true Ivanhoe fashion, contesting the jousting tournaments which surely must have been held there. What the building lacks in history is easily made-up for by imagination, and at this picturesque place the mind can really run free. The Castle Inn was formerly known as The Red Lion, until it was rebuilt in 1885 and renamed. Its story is closely linked to Bodiam Castle and probably came into being in the 15th century when merchants and tradesmen came on

Bodiam Castle

business to the castle. The inn provided the only accommodation for visitors to the village and also catered for the barge traffic which once reached the nearby bridge until the end of last century. Lord Torrington, a visitor in 1780, remarked in his diary that it 'had clean whitewashed walls and only burnt wood on its fires'. Today it provides a cosy watering hole at any time of year.

The parish church of St Giles lies in a picturesque setting half a mile to the north of the castle and is a much restored 14th century building. A former rector was once aide-de-camp to Haile Selassie, and one of the six bells in the tower is named after the Ethiopian emperor.

Hops are grown around Bodiam and before the advent of mechanical picking, the village annually thronged with hop-pickers from London and many other parts of the country, working in the Guinness hopfields.

The disused railway station will soon see a return to service when the Kent and East Sussex Railway re-opens the line from Northiam.

Another colourful attraction at Bodiam are the hot air balloons, which often take off during the summer months when conditions are favourable.

Ewhurst Green

Ewhurst Green is simple but beautiful. The tiny village stands on a sandstone ridge overlooking the River Rother and boasts a delightful pub, historic church, a wealth of attractive weatherboarded cottages and fine examples of converted oasthouses.

The White Dog pub dates from the 17th century and was once called The Castle Inn until the 1960s, when it was re-named after the landlord's dog, to avoid confusion with a pub of the same name at Bodiam.

The 12th century parish church, with its odd-shaped spire, is dedicated to St James the Great and is built of wealden sandstone.

Points of interest inside the church are the 12th century font, an unusual corbel in the north arcade showing a grinning head within a pair of folded arms, and a brass commemorating William Crysford, which dates from 1520.

An ornate corona (chandelier) hangs in the nave and is recognised as the last gift to the church of six-year-old William Jacobson, who was drowned in a pond in his father's garden at nearby Lordine Farm, in 1905.

After his death his parents emptied his money box and made up the amount needed to purchase the corona, providing a lasting memory to their child. There is also a window commemorating the tragedy, showing William sitting on Christ's knee, and above is the face of his mother.

Another sad tale is that of William Goodsell, a resident of nearby Staplecross who, in 1833, was accused of starting a fire in a farm building. He was found guilty at Lewes and later confessed to the crime, saying he was carrying out the wishes of his mother, who bore a grudge against the farmer. He was hanged at Horsham and his body returned to Ewhurst Green for burial.

The beautiful churchyard is a special feature of the village. A carefully planned scheme of planting was carried out between 1942 and 1974, when many varied trees, some rare, were planted. All are clearly marked.

Dr E C Hawtrey, rector between 1835 and 1854 was, at the same time, headmaster of Eton College and in 1916 Lord and Lady Baden Powell were the occupants of nearby Ewhurst Place. Both their children were born there.

Close to Ewhurst Green is the village of Staplecross and a little further south the hamlet of Cripps Corner with its popular White Hart Inn.

Etchingham

Approximately one mile along the road from Hurst Green to Etchingham is Haremere Hall, an early 17th century Manor House, standing in 140 acres of parkland.

The road which winds its way down to Etchingham was originally made during the Napoleonic Wars in the early 1800s, when the existing road, Burgh Hill, proved too steep for horses and carts to transport guns and materials to and from local iron foundries. It was built by navvies, normally employed on canal building and some say they have left their trademark in the unusual way the road is constructed.

Across the Hastings to Charing Cross railway line is the village of Etchingham, once connected with the iron smelting industry. The parish church, dedicated to The Assumption of Blessed Mary and Saint Nicolas, is the main historic point, although there are many fine older buildings in the village. Built from local sandstone by Sir William de Echyngham between 1360 and 1380, the church was originally surrounded by a moat, the remains of which can still be seen.

Among the many interesting features inside the church are the ornate choir stalls with their misericords (ledges under tip-up stalls, to take the weight off the feet during long services), the oldest floor brass in Sussex and a memorial tablet near the south door to Henry Corbould, designer of the Penny Black postage stamp.

The weather vane at the top of the tower, showing the de Echyngham coat of arms, is believed to be the oldest in England and still has its original support.

The local hostelry is the De Etchingham Arms, built in the early 1900s.

*The church weather vane —
the oldest in England*

Burwash

Burwash was once the home of author Rudyard Kipling. It has been described as one of the most enchanting villages in Sussex and its origins date to Norman times, when the manor was given by William the Conqueror to the Count of Eu, in 1096, in recognition of his services in battle.

During the Tudor period Burwash was a thriving centre for the Sussex iron industry and after the demise of iron-making, farming once more became the main industry. Smuggling also played a big part in the life of the village.

Rudyard Kipling's former home, Batemans, lies to the south and was built in 1634 by the ironmaster, John Brittan. Kipling lived at Batemans from 1902 until his death in 1936 and many of his great works were written there. His wife Carrie, who died in 1939, left Batemans to the National Trust as a memorial to her husband. The Trust has meticulously maintained the building through the years and the visitor today can view it more or less as Kipling left it in 1936. The watermill, where the author installed a turbine to provide electricity to the estate, has been restored to full working order and also on show is the Rolls-Royce owned by him between 1928 and 1934. The gardens are a delight and a visit to Batemans is a most fascinating experience. It is open to the public between Easter and October.

The picturesque tree-lined Burwash High Street has many interesting buildings, some dating from before the 16th century. There are good shops, several excellent public houses, quaint tea rooms and a working forge. Burwash has often been judged the best kept village in Sussex.

Batemans

Half way along the street is a map of the village made from ceramic tiles by local artist Eileen Ware. The Manor House of Burghurst stands opposite the church.

The lamp under the cross at the top of the war memorial close to the church is lit on the evening of the anniversary of the death of each serviceman named. Rudyard Kipling's only son, 18-year-old John, who died in France in 1918, is among those remembered.

The Church of Saint Bartholomew was built in 1090 and the tower is all that remains of the original Norman structure. Additions were made in 1190 and 1240 and the church was partly rebuilt and renovated in 1856.

Among the features inside the church are the rare 16th century Geneva Bible, discovered in 1954, among a collection of old books in the vestry of the church, and the John Kipling Memorial by Charles Wheeler, commissioned by Rudyard Kipling. Wheeler went on to become the president of the London Royal Academy of Arts from 1956 till 1966.

Another item with Kipling connections is the cast-iron slab on the wall by the Lady Chapel altar. It is 14th century and was once placed on the floor and formerly marked the last resting place of a member of the local ironmaking family of Collins and is believed to be the oldest example of a Sussex grave slab.

The inscription begins 'Orate p.annnema Jhone Coline' and was the only part Kipling's children were able to decipher. They referred to this part of the church as Panama Corner and Kipling alludes to it in his book 'Rewards and Fairies' in which he re-names the church St Barnabas.

Under the west window of the north aisle is a tablet to Elizabeth Casson, which states she died on February 14 1679/80. The reason for the double year is because it was only in 1752 that a Parliamentary Act was passed to make it legal for the year to commence on January 1. However, before this Act was passed, the year officially began on March 25 and it was often the practice to record dates falling between January 1 and March 25 with both years.

In the .churchyard can be found unusual iron grave markings and several of the tombstones bear the skull and crossbones, reminders of when Burwash was a haven for smuggling in the 18th and 19th centuries.

The road continues westwards through beautiful countryside to the market town of Heathfield, which along with the surrounding villages of Waldron and Mayfield, was the centre of the Sussex iron industry in the 18th century. Also close to Heathfield is the village of Horam, home of the famous Merrydown Cider Company, which is open to the public.

Eastwards to Rye

Fairlight

Reached by turning off the A259 at Ore, on the Hastings outskirts, the village of Fairlight sits loftily on a cliff top and is situated in an area providing some of the finest scenery in the country.

The village is mentioned in records as far back as 1220 as Farlegh, since which date the spelling has had many variations, until 1823 when the present form was adopted. Before the Norman Conquest, the manor belonged to King Harold's father, Earl Godwin and was later granted to the Count of Eu by his cousin, William the Conqueror.

In the 12th century the manor transferred to the Alard family of Winchelsea. Gervase Alard fought in the Crusades and later became Admiral of the Cinque Ports *(see Winchelsea)*.

Fairlight is at the eastern end of Hastings Country Park, an area covering 600 acres which stretches 3½ miles towards Hastings. The park was opened in 1974 and is now a protected conservation area. There is a visitor centre, and through the summer months a programme of guided walks is organised by the Park Rangers.

In the late 19th century the area was a favourite playground for young Archibald Stansfeld Belaney. Born in Hastings in 1888 and educated in the town, Archie had a larger than life fascination for the North American Indian and on reaching the age of 18, he left England for Canada, where he lived as an indian and adopted the name of Grey Owl. During the 1930s he gained worldwide fame as a writer, lecturer and conservationist.

Grey Owl

HM Coastguard Station is positioned close by and at the foot of Fairlight cliffs is the official naturists' beach. Spectating is not considered polite!

Fairlight Glen with its romantic Lovers' Seat was the scene of a true love story in 1786, when the seat was the trysting place of Elizabeth Boys and Captain Charles Lamb. Against their families' wishes the couple eloped to London and married at St Clement's Danes Church in the Strand. Unfortunately, the actual seat is no longer there. It was swept away in a landslip in the 1970s, but the views from the remaining cliffs are breathtaking.

The parish church of St Andrew's stands 563 feet above sea level and its 82ft tower can be seen for miles around and provides an important landmark for shipping. The church was rebuilt in 1845 using stone from a local quarry.

Thomas Attwood Walmisley, a contemporary of Mendelssohn, who became Professor of Music at Cambridge, is buried in the churchyard.

Leaving the church and descending the hill, there is a marked viewpoint, from which can be seen the villages of Pett and Guestling. Mallydams is a bird sanctuary run by the RSPCA and is sometimes open to the public.

Following the main road to the foot of the hill a turning to the right leads to the residential centre of Fairlight. There are more fine cliff top walks, wonderful views and the Fairlight Cove Hotel.

It seems hard to believe that the area of natural beauty surrounding Fairlight was in 1986 threatened with plans by a certain oil company to sink an exploratory well. The uproar was great, an action group was formed and the oil company dropped their plans. Although it did eventually gain permission to drill at a site nearby in 1989, no oil was found.

Pett Level and Pett

Pett Level is situated on a stretch of wild marshland which leads to Winchelsea in the east. In winter it can be a very bleak place, but during the summer months it throngs with life and is a popular venue for many diverse activities, from bathing to birdwatching. There are fine walks and facilities for fishing. The popular Smugglers Inn stands beside the beach.

In 1974 the wreck of the Anne, a British 17th century frigate, was discovered in the sands. It is now a protected site. The vessel was run aground and burnt by her captain in 1690 after a fight with the Dutch off Beachy Head.

Pett Level is also the site of the westermost point of one of the greatest engineering follies ever — The Royal Military Canal, which runs to Hythe in Kent, a distance of some 28 miles.

In 1804, when England was threatened by invasion from Napoleon, it was suggested that a 30ft wide canal should be dug to stop the French. Sir John Rennie, the accomplished engineer, was put in charge of the building by Prime Minister, Sir William Pitt and it was not until the project was near completion that its usefulness was analysed. It was then appreciated, too late, that any army which had crossed the great rivers of Europe, plus the English Channel, would hardly be deterred by a 30ft ditch. The scheme, thought up by an entire government, had cost a staggering £200,000!

The main village of Pett is reached by climbing the steep Chick Hill. It has a pretty mixture of old and new properties and boasts two pubs, The Royal Oak and The Two Sawyers. There is also a small church.

The Two Sawyers was until recent years a private club, and the village was totally void of a pub for over 70 years when The Royal Oak was closed by its Fairlight owner, when she disapproved of over-indulgence by the villagers. She turned it into a temperance hotel and banned drink. However, the situation is now entirely back to normal!

The grave of 'Alice'

ALFRED HENRY
BROCKWELL
DIED 26TH NOV 1973
AGED 83 YEARS.
ALSO
OLIVE CHRISTINE
BROCKWELL
WIFE OF THE ABOVE
REUNITED 26TH APRIL 1978
AGED 83 YEARS
SHE WAS THE 'ALICE' OF A A MILNE'S
CHRISTOPHER ROBIN BOOKS

Guestling

Guestling is situated on the A259. Named Ghestlinges in the Domesday Book, it gave its name to one of the three ancient administrational courts which managed the affairs of the Cinque Ports. The Court of Brotherhood and Guestling still formally meets each year.

The most influential local family in the 15th century were the Ashburnhams, when Richard Ashburnham married the daughter of Sir John Stonelink and inherited the mansion and estate known as Broomham. There are memorials in the Ashburnham Chapel in the parish church.

The church, parts of which date from the late Saxon period, is signposted off the A259 and situated at a bend in the narrow lane beside a farm. It is dedicated to St Laurence, martyred in 258 AD by the Romans, who disbelieved his claim that he spent all the riches of the church on the poor and needy. The tower, doorway and archway of the church date to Norman times. The building was extensively restored after 1890 when a serious fire did much damage to the interior. The dark smoke-stains caused by the fire can still be seen today. A chained copy of Foxe's Book of Martyrs, produced in 1685, is on display.

Another influential local family were the Cheyneys, whose memorial can be found to the left of the altar. Elizabeth, who died in 1603, left cottages as homes for widows from Guestling and Icklesham *(see Icklesham)*.

Buried in the churchyard is Olive Christine Brockwell, who died in 1978, aged 83. She was better known as the nanny Alice of Changing the Guard fame. A fresh inscription on her gravestone was added by Christopher Milne (the original Christopher Robin), son of the author and creator, A A Milne.

In 1848 Guestling was the scene of three shocking murders, when Mary Ann Geering poisoned her husband and two of her 10 children with arsenic. They are buried in the churchyard in unmarked graves. The much-disturbed Mary Ann had intended to kill the whole family, but with three dead, the local doctor became suspicious and ordered the exhumation of her victims, when traces of the arsenic were found. She was arrested, found guilty and hanged at Lewes in August 1849, before a crowd of 4000 onlookers.

To the north of the village, the house known as Maxfield was the birthplace of 16th century scholar Gregory Martin, responsible for translating the Latin Bible into English. He died in 1582 and is buried in France.

Brick-making has always been a local industry and today in Fourteen Acre Lane, the Hastings Brickworks supplies specialist hand-made bricks for restoration work on churches and other old buildings. Among the company's more famous customers are Buckingham Palace and Hampton Court and its products were used at Camber Castle.

Eastwards the A259 passes the Manor House of Broomham, now a public school, and a turning to the left leads to the hamlet of Three Oaks, and its attractive inn, which falls within the parish boundary.

Icklesham

Eastwards along the A259 from Guestling is the village of Icklesham. The earliest known reference to Icklesham is dated 772, when the Saxon Charter of King Offa of Mercia records that a gift of three hides of land be given to Bishop Oswald of the see of Selsey. A hide was 'as much land as could be tilled with one plough in a year'. The Charter, written in Latin, gave the name of the manor as Ikelesham, the Anglo-Saxon translation being Icoleshamme, meaning 'the homestead of the family Icel'.

Icklesham may have been one of the first places in England to be occupied by the Normans when William the Conqueror seized the Hastings Peninsula. The village had great strategic importance. Before the late 13th century the parish of Icklesham included the hill on which the new town of Winchelsea was built and stretched to the mouth of the River Rother.

The magnificent Parish Church of All Saints, a place of worship for over 800 years, bears witness to the skill and craftsmanship of its builders and is well worth a long visit. The giant pillars and arches in the nave are fine examples of Norman building dating from the 12th century. The church has been added to and restored, and has a rich variety of architectural styles. The carved stone corbels on the chancel arch date from the 13th century and carved crosses on the western pillars were made by soldiers of the Crusades.

On the north wall is a noticeboard showing two early charities in the parish, still in existence today: The Cheyney Trust and the John Fray bequest of 1592. The widow Elizabeth Cheyney left 'half an acre of land and two tenements for the use of two poor and aged unmarried men or women' in 1710. Although both charities are still applicable, the monies received from the bequests hold the same value as they did 400 years ago. A large sum then, but mere shillings today!

Icklesham is one of the few Sussex parishes which made evacuation plans in the event of the feared invasion from France during the Napoleonic Wars. In 1798 detailed returns were made of livestock and provisions and all persons, young and old were made aware of the possibility of compulsory movement from their homes and instructions were issued on what to do in the event of attack. However, as history tells us, they were not needed.

The Oast public house was originally built in the reign of Henry VIII and nearby, at the end of a lane, is the splendid 17th century Queen's Head.

To the east of the village can be seen the smock windmill on Hog's Hill, which today is used by ex-Beatle, Paul McCartney, as a recording studio.

'A town in a trance, a sunny dream of centuries ago'. So said of Winchelsea by Victorian poet Coventry Patemore. The same reflections would appear to be valid today. It is beautifully maintained, clean, unrushed and as pretty as a picture with an air of quality and prosperity. It is the next stop along the A259 from Icklesham and is well worth exploring.

The town has a long and fascinating history. The portion which remains today is in fact not the original Winchelsea at all. The first town was situated three miles south-east from its present position on a shingle spur and may have been an important port as early as Roman times.

It was certainly of great importance in Saxon times. They gave the place its name 'the shingle isle on the level' and in 959 the town was important enough to possess a mint.

In the 11th century the town was given to the Abbey of Fecamp, along with Rye, Hastings and other manors in the area and it was at Winchelsea that William the Conqueror landed in December 1067 when returning from Normandy for the first time after the Conquest. During the 12th century the 'Antient Town of Winchelsea' became a prominent member of the Cinque Ports and continued to grow in importance, prestige and prosperity. But then followed a series of catastrophies!

The first was natural. A great storm in 1250 severely damaged the port and in 1287 the town was finally swept away completely. King Edward I, realising its importance, ordered the building of a new town on the present site, the high point of Iham, then almost totally surrounded by sea. The new Winchelsea was a planner's dream. The initial intention was to fill 39 squares on a spacious grid pattern, but in the event only about a dozen of the squares were ever built upon.

Now safe from the sea, the town was then subjected to its second disaster, this time man-made. At intervals during the 14th and early 15th centuries, the town was ransacked by invading French marauders, whose raids caused much death and destruction. On the first of the raids a hundred houses were burned down and the church attacked, and in 1359, 3000 French invaders breached the town wall and raided the church, which being Sunday was full. They butchered all within their path and desecrated the church. The graveyard of St

Giles Church (nothing remains of the church today), had to be enlarged to accommodate the victims of the attack. A narrow lane runs close to the site of the old church and churchyard. It is aptly known as Deadman's Lane and provides a reminder of that dreadful day. It is said that no birds sing there, the trees block the sun and is understandably believed to be one of the most haunted places in the country.

In all there were seven attacks from the French during the 14th and 15th centuries. There were later reprisals as the men of Winchelsea sailed the Channel to mete their revenge on the town of Petershaven in Normandy.

The third decisive blow to the town came from its old adversary, the sea. Having destroyed the original Winchelsea, it now began to retreat resulting in the silting of the harbour. By the 16th century Winchelsea was marooned and had lost its importance as a port and the town fell slowly but steadily into decay. The Methodist preacher, John Wesley, described it in 1790 as 'That poor skeleton of Ancient Winchelsea'.

During the 18th century it became a haunt for smugglers, the large cellars making ideal hiding places for contraband. The illicit trade continued until the early 19th century.

As a Cinque Port, Winchelsea held the privilege of returning two members of Parliament. There was considerable corruption as men paid large sums to obtain a seat in the House. This all came to an end in 1832, when both members were discharged on the introduction of the Reform Act.

Until 1876 the town was governed by the Mayor and Corporation from the old Court Hall, when the Municipal Corporations Act took these powers away. However, as a prominent member of the Cinque Ports, Winchelsea was allowed to keep its Mayor and Corporation and still does to this day.

By the 19th century Winchelsea began to re-emerge from its depression as the town became popular with artists and writers, such as Turner, Thackeray and Patemore. The actress Ellen Terry lived at Tower Cottage from 1896 until 1906. The town began to take on a smarter image by fostering a more cultural approach and promoting interest in its past.

In 1975 with the National Trust's acquisition of land surrounding the village the area is now protected and fully recognised for its important historic contribution.

Winchelsea today covers only a fraction of the original site. An indication of its initial size can be gauged by noting the positions of the remains of the three original medieval gates.

The New Gate, the furthest from the town centre, surrounded by trees and the town ditch (an addition to the town's defences), is to the south of the town. It was through this gate that the French are said to have gained access in 1380.

The Pipewell or Land Gate is the newest and stands at the north-east of the town at the side of the busy A259. It was rebuilt in 1404 by the Mayor of Winchelsea. His shield can be seen on the structure. The gate had been destroyed by the French in 1380.

The most imposing and best-preserved is Strand Gate at the sea end of the town. It was built in the late 13th century and the steep hill once led down to Winchelsea Harbour. The arch was once fortified by a portcullis, the grooves of which can still be seen.

The Look Out close to the gate provides breathtaking views across to Romney Marsh and Rye and the Dungeness Power Station can be seen on the horizon. At the foot of the hill, a section of the Grand Military Canal can be seen *(see Pett)*.

The Court Hall is one of the oldest buildings in the town, but was extensively restored during Tudor times. The local museum is housed on the upper floor and the lower rooms were once the town prison. The museum contains many interesting exhibits illustrating the history of the Cinque Ports and there is a detailed model of the town as it was in its original form. There is also a list of Mayors dating from 1245. The Mayor-making ceremony is held on Easter Monday and is open to the public. For 700 years this ancient tradition has been proudly preserved.

The parish church of St Thomas the Martyr is quite magnificent and, in my humble opinion, the most beautiful church in the area. When stepping inside, it is difficult to appreciate you are visiting a small town, such are the cathedral-like proportions and atmosphere within. The stunning modern stained glass windows are remarkable.

The church is the surviving easternmost part of the original building erected between 1288 and 1292. In its original state it was a cruciform building of considerable size, but was partly destroyed by the French in the 14th century and never rebuilt. The ruins of the transepts of the original building can still be seen and give the church a quite unique appearance.

The main attraction in the church is the Alard Chantry in the south aisle, a memorial to the renowned ancient Winchelsea family. The monument to Gervase Alard, who was the first British Admiral and Warden of the Cinque Ports at the beginning of the 14th century, is a striking feature.

Among the beautiful stained glass windows is one commemorating the bravery of the Rye Harbour lifeboat crew who lost their lives in 1928 *(see Rye Harbour)*. It is the work of Douglas Strachan and was unveiled in 1929.

The church is crammed with items of interest and if you do nothing else while in Winchelsea, make sure you visit this beautiful place.

Standing by the outer wall of the church close to the road, opposite the New Inn, is Wesley's Tree, where the great preacher gave his last open-air sermon in 1790. The original tree survived until 1927 and the one standing there now was grown from a cutting from the original. Wesley also preached at the nearby Methodist Chapel in 1785.

The building known as the Barracks was built in 1763 and housed troops during the Napoleonic Wars, when Winchelsea was an army headquarters. At this time The Duke of Wellington stayed at Tower Cottage while reviewing the troops. The names of the streets and houses reflect the army connection.

The Armoury in Barrack Square was a public house in the 18th century known as The Bear Inn. A bear pit is said to have been situated adjacent.

The old town well has an original sign above, dated July 1872, which states that any person throwing anything whatever down the well may be prosecuted.

Winchelsea once had six open wells from which people drew their water. It is said that anyone who drinks the water of St Leonard's Well 'Shall never leave Winchelsea. Wherever he roams his heart is still there'. It is situated at the bottom of the cliff to the north-west of the town.

The Salutation Inn has not opened its doors as a pub for many years, but the old cellar entrance can still be seen in the wall where Mill Road joins Castle Street. Badly damaged by a German bomb in 1943, it was later repaired and the name has survived.

Today, Winchelsea is served by the picturesque 18th century New Inn and The Bridge Inn, which is situated at the bottom of the hill on the road to Rye.

Winchelsea once had three hospitals for the old and infirm. The remains of St John's Hospital can be seen at the edge of the town on the Icklesham road.

In the grounds of Greyfriars, now a home for the elderly, are the beautiful ruins of the Franciscan Chapel of the Blessed Virgin and on the other side of the town, close to the cricket field, are the remains of a house which belonged to the Black Friars, who came to Winchelsea in 1318. This part of the town was once built up and the large ditch is evidence of the siting of the town wall on the far side of the cricket field.

Winchelsea is served by British Rail and the station is about a mile away.

Rye Harbour

Off the A259 to the west of Rye is the tiny village of Rye Harbour. Today it is a popular holiday centre, where small boats of all descriptions can be seen.

In the churchyard is a sad reminder of the cruelty and unpredictability of the sea. In 1928 the close-knit fishing community was devastated by one of the worst disasters ever to befall the Royal National Lifeboat Institution, when the entire crew of 17 men of *The Mary Stanford* lifeboat, was lost when the boat overturned in heavy seas on November 15. A memorial to the men stands over the mass grave. The boathouse from which *The Mary Stanford* sailed on that fateful night still stands on the lonely stretch of beach a mile-and-a-half from the village and can be reached by taking the walkway along the side of the harbour. A full size lifeboat was never stationed again at Rye Harbour after the disaster and today an inshore craft patrols the area.

Close to the old boathouse is Rye Harbour Nature Reserve where birds of every description can be viewed from hides.

Inland to the west is Camber Castle, built by Henry VIII. It was erected to guard Rye Bay and the sea once reached its outer limits. It has recently undergone restoration.

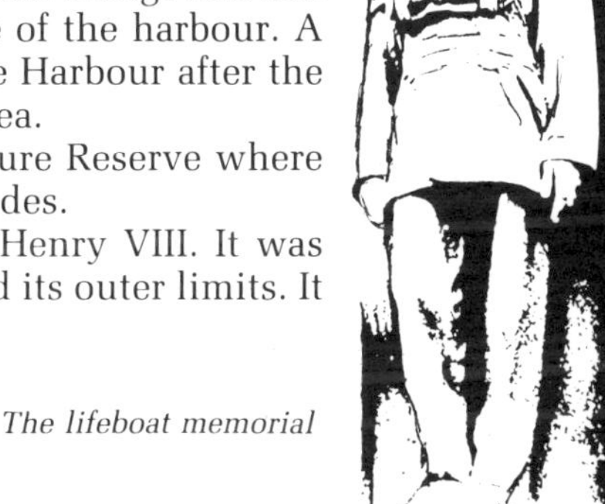

The lifeboat memorial

Rye

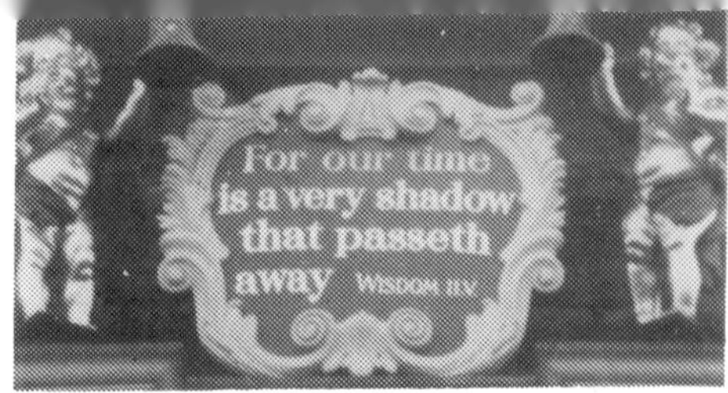

The Quarter Boys

Rye is situated about two miles east of Winchelsea and is arguably the most beautiful town in the country. Standing high on a sandstone rock, its cobbled streets and half-timbered houses are an artist's (or photographer's) dream and a delight for historians. Many times its picturesque streets have been used in the making of films and television series. Small wonder it is in the top ten of every foreign visitor's holiday in England and that each year thousands pour into the town. Every corner holds a delightful surprise and Rye is the jewel in East Sussex's crown! It has something for everyone.

Rye has a population of 5000 and far from being just 'a pretty face', a historic time capsule or museum preserved to attract tourists, it is a busy market town with good shopping facilities and businesses. As well as tourism, the town supports boat-building, fishing, pottery-making and light industry and a cattle market is held every Wednesday and general market every Thursday.

There is ample car parking away from the town centre and a town bus runs regularly from the immediate outskirts. Rye is served by British Rail with trains to Hastings in the west and Ashford in the east.

Rye is built on a hilltop at the end of the Southern Ridge and originally the sea came much closer to the town. In pre-Roman times a ridgeway led from the estuary at Rye, inland to mid-Sussex. The Romans built a road, which was used for the movement of iron.

In AD 500 the area was inhabited by the Saxons and Jutes of northern Europe and later by the unruly Danes, who were finally brought to order by King Alfred the Great.

In the 11th century Rye and its neighbour, the old port of Winchelsea, were part of the Manor of Rameslie and given to the Abbey of Fecamp by King Canute. The towns were later joined to the Federation of Cinque Ports, firstly as 'limbs' of Hastings, and later as full members in the 13th century.

During the great storms of 1287 old Winchelsea was submerged, but due to its hilly position Rye survived, although the eastern and lower parts of the town were lost to the sea in 1380. Gradually the sea receded and the River Rother, originally known as the Limen, changed its course to flow to the sea at Rye. The town remained an important port and market town during the 13th and 14th centuries and by the 15th century was considered to have the best harbour of all the Cinque Ports.

During the 14th and 15th centuries Rye was subjected to frequent attacks from the French, the worst being in 1377, when much of the town was destroyed. The French raids continued and the town was largely rebuilt in the 16th century and it is these buildings which are so well preserved today.

In 1573 Queen Elizabeth I visited and legend says she gave her royal approval by bestowing the title 'Rye Royal' on the town. In 1590 and 1596 Rye was decimated by the plague.

By the 16th century the wide harbour had begun to silt up and slowly the landscape changed, but until the early 1800s the sea still covered the area known today as The Salts.

In the 18th century Rye became a Borough and returned two members to parliament. Arthur Wellesley (later The Duke of Wellington) was the best known. Rye continued to elect two members until the Reform Act of 1832.

There are so many interesting things to see in Rye, it is difficult to know where to start. A walk round Rye can take as little or as long as you like. Be prepared for plenty of diversions! The streets are packed with 'olde worlde' tea rooms, pubs and restaurants. The town also has a reputation for pottery and there are several good quality antique shops.

The huge Landgate was built in the middle of the 14th century and is the only remaining gateway through the old town wall which once fortified the town. The clock was added in 1863 to commemorate Prince Albert.

Many fine old buildings can be seen in High Street, among them the Apothecary Shop and Old Grammar School. The school was founded in 1636 by Thomas Peacocke. A modern school on the outskirts of the town still bears his name. The George Hotel dates from the 17th century.

In Conduit Hill, which runs off the High Street, are the ruins of an Augustinian Friary, built in 1379.

The Church of St Mary the Virgin is situated on the town's highest point. The gilded Quarter Boys stand either side of the ornate clock and, as their name suggests, strike the quarter hours (but not the hours). The figures are replicas made of fibre glass — the originals are stored inside the church.

St Mary's dates from 1120 and there are some Norman remains, despite the sacking of the church by the French in 1377. There are interesting features within the church, the most spectacular being the oldest turret clock in the country with its 18ft pendulum swinging above the congregation. It was made at Winchelsea and has been working for 400 years. It cost £31! The clock tower is open to the public during the summer months and affords wonderful views.

The beautiful churchyard and surrounding square give the impression of stepping back in time. Many fine buildings of all architectural periods grace Church Square.

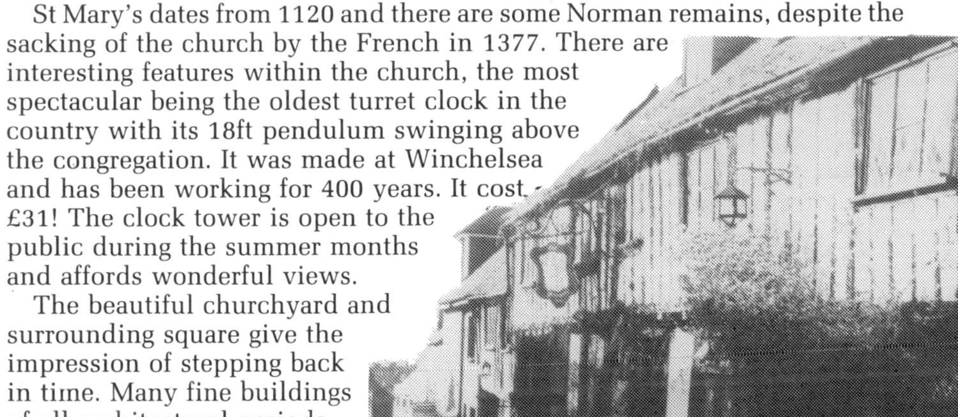

Mermaid Hotel

The Old Custom House, with its crooked chimney, dates from the 15th century and is the place Elizabeth I stayed when visiting Rye in 1573. On the eastern side of Church Square is an unusual oval Water House, built in 1735 to provide water from its pure wells. A scandal occurred in 1754 when a nearby butcher's shop in Market Street polluted the pipes. Calves feet were found in them!

Ypres Tower houses the renowned Rye Museum. Built in 1250 as a fortification, by order of Henry III, Ypres Tower served as a prison for 400 years until 1865 and later as a mortuary.

The views from Gungarden, across the marshes to the sea, are impressive. The cannons commemorate the visit of Queen Elizabeth, the Queen Mother.

The Town Hall is a beautiful Georgian building, which contains the maces and mayoral chain of office. Mayoring Day is still celebrated annually, when the odd custom of throwing hot pennies from the Town Hall windows to children in the street below, is still observed.

An odd possession kept in the Town Hall is the gruesome gibbet cage containing the skull of murderer, Butcher Breads. Breads was hung in 1743. He had long borne a grudge against local mayor and magistrate, James Lamb, who had earlier fined him for giving short weight, and one night he set out to kill him.

However, in the darkness of the churchyard at midnight, he stabbed Lamb's brother-in-law Allen Grebell, by mistake. The unfortunate Grebell had been standing in for his brother-in-law at a function and had borrowed his red mayoral cloak. After being stabbed he struggled home, told his manservant he felt unwell and bled to death in front of the fire during the night. Breads was eventually arrested after dancing drunkenly through the streets shouting 'Butchers should kill lambs'. James Lamb, his intended victim, presided at the trial. Say no more!

The skull is all that remains. The rest of the bones were stolen. It was believed that soup made from them would cure rheumatism! The ghosts of Butcher Breads and Alan Grebell are said to haunt the churchyard.

The council treasures and Breads' skull are occasionally on show by arrangement with the Mayor's office.

Breads' former home, The Flushing Inn, now a restaurant, dates from around 1450 and underneath is an early cellar dated around 1100. In the restaurant is a wall painting dating from the 16th century.

Lamb House was built in the 18th century by James Lamb, a member of the wealthy Rye family which served the mayoralty many times. In 1726 George I was a visitor to the house when his ship was driven ashore at Camber. On the first night of his stay, James Lamb's wife gave birth to a son. The baby was later baptised George with the king as his godfather.

Rye has been the residence of many writers and artists through the years. Perhaps the most famous was Henry James. Lamb House was once the home

Church Square

of the American author and during his occupancy nearly every writer of note made visits to the house, among them Rudyard Kipling and H G Wells.

The famous brothers, A C and E F Benson later resided at Lamb House. A C Benson wrote the words to 'Land of Hope and Glory' and E F Benson was the creator of the infamous Miss Mapp. Rye was named as Tilling in his stories. Prunella Scales played Miss Mapp in the successful television series 'Mapp and Lucia', which was made on location in Rye. The series also starred Nigel Hawthorne and Geraldine McEwan.

Lamb House is now run by The National Trust and is open to the public. The detached garden room where Henry James wrote many of his novels was destroyed by a German bomb in 1940.

A top favourite with tourists, especially Americans, is 15th century Mermaid Inn. Standing in the picturesque, much filmed, Mermaid Street, it has dark beams, panellings and an enormous fireplace. It is easy to imagine the smugglers congregating there in the heyday of their illicit trading, which was particularly prevalent in Rye. The Methodist preacher John Wesley, a frequent visitor to Rye, recorded in his diary: 'The good people will not part with the accursed thing — smuggling.'

In the same street is Hartshorn House, formerly a hospital. The half-timbered building dates from the 16th century.

At the foot of Mermaid Street is Strand Quay, where the Rye Heritage Centre, houses a model of the town with a sound and light show illustrating the history. It was in this part of Rye that the huge Strand Gate once stood.

The Strand Quay is the scene of tasteful development and is a very atmospheric part of Rye, where many boats can be seen.

The road named The Mint returns to High Street. Coins were minted in Rye in the 12th century.

Rye has many ghost stories. The most famous tells of a monk with a lovely singing voice who fell in love with a beautiful local girl. After eloping, they were caught and the punishment was to be bricked up alive in a wall. The ghost of the monk, whose beautiful voice turned into the gobble of a turkey, can be seen and heard in Turkey Cock Lane.

There are so many good public houses in and around Rye, it's impossible to name them all. However, a personal favourite and one which often escapes attention because of its distance from the town centre, is the excellent Top o' the Hill on the road to Playden.

The Top o' the Hill

East Guldeford and Camber

These two contrasting places are situated at the most eastern points of East Sussex and illustrate the extremes to be found. East Guldeford, a tiny hamlet and Camber, a bustling, thriving holiday resort.

East Guldeford (pronounced Gilford), situated on the A259 east of Rye, is possibly the loneliest, most wind-swept settlement in the county, nestling on the edge of Romney Marsh. In the 15th century much of the marshland was salt and the substance provided the area with a thriving industry.

The isolated barn-like church is situated in a field and was built in 1505 by Sir Richard Guldeford, whose family took their name from the city of Guildford. It is built of Tudor brick and was carefully restored in the 1970s. The church has the unusual feature of twin roofs with a bell-cote between and inside are box pews and a double decked pulpit.

Sir Richard also built a sea wall and drained the area to transform it into farmland. A ferry was in operation in 1500 when the area was enclosed by the sea and continued working until the 19th century.

Although there is little other than the church to see at East Guldeford, it is the gateway to the Romney Marshes, stretching to the east, an area immortalised by the famous Dr Syn books of Russell Thorndike. His tales of the pirating and smuggling vicar captured the imagination of millions.

The Romney Marshes abound with stories of smuggling and there is much to explore in the quaint little towns and villages. If it's solitude, peace and quiet you are looking for, this area certainly fits the bill.

Camber, on the other hand, is quite the reverse. Reached by following the signs off the A259 or by a bracing two mile walk from Rye, Camber has miles of fine, golden sand, amusement arcades and many modern day attractions.

The 18-hole Rye Golf Course is one of the finest in the country and covers about 3¼ miles. It is the venue each January for the Oxford and Cambridge varsity golf match.

There is also a large leisure park which offers a wide choice of accommodation, caravans and chalets. It has a heated indoor swimming pool, bars and restaurant.

Until the Second World War a steam tram linked Camber to Rye and during the war it was used for military purposes. A ferry once took passengers across the estuary to Rye Harbour. It was operated by ex-fisherman, Johnny Doughty, who achieved fame as a folk singer, at the age of 74. He released an album of his local songs in 1976 and made several appearances on radio and television. He died in 1985, aged 82 and is buried in Rye. His boat featured in the film 'Green Grow The Rushes', which starred Robert Beatty and Jane Wyman, a fact never forgotten by the locals.

The 1950s movie 'Dunkirk', was made at Camber Sands.

Camber Castle *(see Rye Harbour)* is not actually at Camber, but is situated some distance to the west, a point which confuses many a visitor.

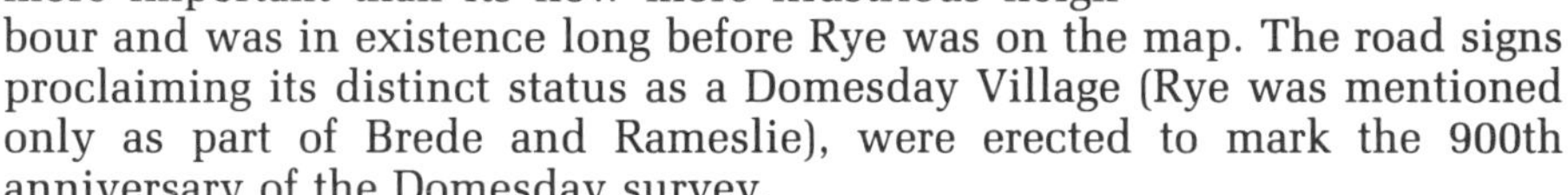

Playden and Iden

Standing half a mile to the north of Rye, the village of Playden has fierce pride in the fact that it was once more important than its now more illustrious neighbour and was in existence long before Rye was on the map. The road signs proclaiming its distinct status as a Domesday Village (Rye was mentioned only as part of Brede and Rameslie), were erected to mark the 900th anniversary of the Domesday survey.

After the Norman Conquest, the manor was named Pleidenam in the Domesday Book and was held by the Count of Eu. The present hill-top church with its eyecatching cedar-shingled spire (slightly crooked if viewed from the east), was started on the site of a wooden Saxon church in 1190 and is dedicated to St Michael.

Features inside include a carved oak screen, dating from 1310, considered to be the church's finest possession, and a small black stone slab, dated 1530, marking the last resting place of Flemish brewer, Cornelis Roetmans. The carboniferous limestone slab, imported from Belgium, is inscribed with the insignia of the brewer's trade. Originally the drawings were inlaid in brass.

Playden once enjoyed prosperity as a fish salting centre, when fish were spread on the sides of the road to dry. This earned it the name Saltcote or the corruption, Sauket Street, a name used until the 18th century. In the 14th century the village had a leper hospital within its boundaries.

Hostelries in the village are The Peace and Plenty and The Playden Oast.

A mile to the east is Iden, another place proud of its Domesday heritage.

It overlooks the marshes and the Royal Military Canal lies within the southern boundary. The Iden Lock and original lock cottage is situated where the canal joins the River Rother.

The village once had a castellated house, surrounded by a moat. It was built in 1284 by Edmund de Paseley and known as The Motes and was later the home of Alexander Iden, Sheriff of Sussex in the 15th century. All that remains today is a portion of the gateway, but the outlines of the moat can still clearly be seen.

The village has two pubs. The Bell, in the centre of the village, was built in 1107 and was originally a dwelling for the monks during the building of the nearby church.

The Parish Church of All Saints, with its castellated belltower, dates from the 11th century but has been much restored. Only two rectors served the church in the 117 years between 1807 and 1924, a fact noted in the Guinness Book of Records.

Until recently the village had a jam-making factory. Started as a small cottage industry in 1929 by Miss Dorothy Carter, the Still Room flourished and grew into a successful company supplying prestigious outlets such as Fortnum & Mason from its tiny premises in Reader Lane.

Peasmarsh

As the A268 road from Rye approaches Peasmarsh, it passes through the hamlet of Rye Foreign. Its name is derived from the French Huguenots who, on fleeing their own country, settled in the area. Opposite the Hare and Hounds pub is an incredibly odd but very eye-catching structure, called Cordbat Cottage. The name cordbat means a pile of logs. Most apt!

Peasmarsh, an iron-smelting centre in Roman times, has no proper village centre and the parish church is situated some distance away. It is said this points to the possibility that an earlier settlement was wiped out by the Black Death. Whatever the reason, the Church of St Peter and St Paul is set in a beautiful, isolated meadow, off Church Lane.

There is much of the original building remaining, which dates from 1070 and the chancel arch, built of iron-sandstone, has remained almost untouched since Norman times. Once, the displaying of the Ten Commandments, The Creed and the Lord's Prayer (the Triptych) was a compulsory requirement for every parish church and the original example above the chancel arch dates from Elizabethan times.

A strange story was told to me, concerning the memorial window to Helen, the wife of the Rev W R Brodrick, a former rector of the church. It is dated 1863 and dedicated to her memory by the Rev W R ICK. Far from it being a nickname or the fact that the engraver was trying to save space, the story goes that the reverend gentleman thought himself due a family windfall and when it failed to fully materialise, he changed his name by deducting a letter to symbolise each thousand pounds he felt his inheritance had fallen short!

Nearby is Peasmarsh Place, a Georgian house, once the home of the Liddell family. The Very Rev H G Liddell was Dean of Christ Church Oxford. His son helped to compile the Liddell and Scott's Greek Dictionary and his daughter Alice was the inspiration for Lewis Carroll's Alice in Wonderland. Peasmarsh Place is now a care home for the elderly.

William Pattison, born in the village in 1706, was a gifted poet, but he was certainly not a winner! He just didn't seem to be able to get anything right. He built up debts while still at school, entered Cambridge University, was threatened with expulsion but left of his own accord and died at the age of 21. If that wasn't bad enough, his poetry caused great offence. Victorian author M A Lower said of his poetry, most of which was written in his teenage years, that 'it showed a moral depravity'. Today's most famous and gifted resident is songwriter Paul McCartney, who lives close to the village.

A must for the connoisseur of pub grub is the Horse and Cart public house.

Beckley

The village of Beckley is situated off the A268 Peasmarsh to Northiam road and its main street (one of the longest in Sussex), containing many fine Georgian houses, is an architectural delight.

In the 9th century the village belonged to King Alfred the Great, who left it to his kinsman, Osferthe. It was then known by the name of Beccanleah.

The woodlands surrounding Beckley have been the site of iron workings since Roman times but it was in the 17th and 18th centuries that the industry reached its peak, when Beckley Furnace specialised in the manufacture of cannons for use all over the world. Production began in 1653.

During the 18th century difficulties were experienced in working the furnace due to the shortage of water needed to power the bellows. When this occurred men had to tread the waterwheel, to keep the furnace blowing and maintain production. The iron works finally closed down in 1770.

Occasionally pieces of glassware are dug up in the area, which suggests that glassmaking was another industry pursued in bygone days.

The beautiful ancient church of All Saints was built in the 12th century on the site of a former Saxon building and the parish registers date from 1697, although the list of rectors dates from Laurence de London in 1245.

The table tombstones close to the churchyard fence once stood inside the church. They belong to former 17th century rector, the Rev Thomas Sharpe, his wife and son. The Rev Sharpe lived at Church House opposite and was brought to trial in Cromwellian times for continuing to use the Prayer Book Service. Before his trial at Lewes, both he and his wife were so severely beaten by Cromwell's troops, that Mrs Sharpe died from her injuries.

The dug out chest inside the church is thought to be 12th century and was dug out of one tree-trunk. It has some of the earliest ironwork in the county attached to it. It is believed it once held church treasures and could only be opened by three keyholders, who all had to be in attendance.

A local legend concerning the church states that one of the murderers of Thomas a Beckett tried to gain sanctuary at the church, his right hand still stained with the blood of his victim. In his confusion the knight had forgotten that to treason and sacrilege the Privilege of Sanctuary meant he could never be given safety in Beckley church — or anywhere else for that matter. His ghost and that of his horse are said to haunt the village at night.

A mile away on the A268 Rye to Northiam road is a modern day attraction — The Great Knelle Children's Farm where youngsters can get a close-up view of the animals and help to participate in the working of the farm.

Beckley has a good selection of shops and is served by two public houses. The Royal Oak is on the village green and The Rose and Crown, once a coaching inn on the London to Rye road, is at the western end of the village.

Great Dixter

Northiam

On the road from Beckley to Northiam, is the large Manor House known as Brickwall. Built in 1490 this impressive timbered house was for 400 years the home of the influential Frewen family and is now a private school for dyslexic boys. The grounds are open to the public during summer months and the gardens, laid out by Jane Frewen in the 18th century contain plants from around the world. There is also an early bowling green and a section of the garden where yew trees are being grown to the shape of chess pieces.

Northiam has an abundance of old buildings surrounding the picturesque green and is widely regarded as one of the prettiest villages in East Sussex.

The ornate pump supplied water to the village until 1907 and it was under the nearby Elizabeth oak that Good Queen Bess is reputed to have taken refreshment while on a journey to Rye in 1573. It is said she dined on a meal prepared at the nearby Hayes Hotel, a former farmhouse. In the original Tudor section can be seen the huge inglenook fireplace containing the bake-oven where the queen's meal was cooked. She left her green damask shoes as a memento to the people of the village.

The parish church stands on one of the highest points in the village and dates from the 12th century, although only the lower part of the tower and the west wall remain from the original building. There are very few examples of this type of octagonal stone spire to be found in Sussex.

There is much evidence of the influence the Frewen family had on the village and the church. It was beneath the St Nicholas Chapel that the first Frewen family vault was built in the reign of Charles II. In 1738 a second vault was added with an entrance and steps from the churchyard but even this was not sacred to smugglers. Contraband was often stored among the coffins until the entrance was bricked up in 1786 and the iron gates surrounding the vault were removed. In 1846 the impressive Frewen Mausoleum was built to cover the vault.

John Frewen, rector in 1583, in true Puritan tradition, named his first two sons Accepted and Thankful. Accepted was outlawed by Cromwell with a price of £1000 on his head, but later became Archbishop of York in 1660 and is buried in York Minster. Another Archbishop of York with Northiam connections is John Sharpe, who served in 1691.

In 1944, four Prime Ministers, Winston Churchill of Great Britain,

Mackenzie King of Canada, Jan Christian Smuts of South Africa and Godfrey Huggins of Southern Rhodesia met on the playing fields opposite the Crown and Thistle public house to inspect the troops prior to D-Day. Their names are inscribed on the gates which were erected to commemorate the event.

There is a wealth of fine old houses in the Northiam area, but the most famous is the timber-framed Great Dixter. The original house was built in 1450. It was bought by Nathanial Lloyd in 1910, and later restored by Sir Edward Lutyens, when he transported a derelict 16th century house piece by piece from Benenden in Kent to Great Dixter and reassembled it on the south side of the original house. Lutyens also laid out the garden, and with contributions from Nathanial Lloyd and more recently from Christopher Lloyd, the garden has now become one of the top show gardens in the south. The house and gardens are open to the public between April and October.

In stark contrast to Great Dixter is Smuggler's Cottage, reputed to be the smallest house in Sussex. It is situated on the main A28 road and is said to have once housed a family of five.

The newly refurbished railway station is situated 1½ miles out of the village. The railway returned to Northiam after a gap of 36 years and is run by the Kent and East Sussex Railway which operates from nearby Tenterden. The refurbishment of the station formed 'The Challenge' for Anneka Rice in her popular BBC television programme in 1989. A few yards further along the A28 is the border with Kent and the picturesque village of Newenden.

Leaving Northiam in the Hastings direction, after a-mile-and-a-half the A28 passes a sign post to a catholic church. There is an interesting story connected to this church and it is worth taking the short diversion to see it. The founder was authoress Sheila Kaye-Smith, who once owned the nearby oasthouse, Little Doucegrove.

Born in Hastings, she lived most of her life in the district and was a deeply religious woman whose novels reflected her initial Anglo-Catholic beliefs. Many of her works include reference to her beloved part of Sussex.

In 1924 she married Penrose Fry, the curate at Christ Church, St Leonards but soon began to question her beliefs and felt the desire to become a full Catholic. After moving to Little Doucegrove, both she and her husband were received into the Catholic church in 1929.

As Little Doucegrove was almost 10 miles from the nearest Catholic church, she converted a loft over the stables into a chapel which she called the Upper Room and a priest held Mass there at quarterly intervals. The Mass soon became a weekly event and as the congregation outgrew the oratory, she made available land and money to build a small church nearby. In 1935 the Church of St Therese of Lisieux was opened. The first priest, Father Currie, was incumbent there until 1983.

Sheila Kaye-Smith died after a fall at her home and is buried in the graveyard of the church she instigated. It is a beautiful, tranquil spot.

Udimore

Udimore is reached by the B2089 from Broad Oak and stands on a high ridge overlooking the Brede and Tillingham Valleys. It is an attractive setting with many charming properties and spectacular country views across the Brede Level to the sea in the south and the beautiful Tillingham Valley to the north. In bygone days both valleys were vast inlets of the sea. From Norman times, land was slowly reclaimed over the years by draining the marshy areas with dikes (a process known as 'inning') but until as late as the 1930s barges sailed as far inland as Brede.

According to legend the village gained its name from the angels! When the building of the first church was about to start, not on its present site but on marshy land to the south, the angels intervened and the foundations which were laid each day mysteriously disappeared each night until the curious parishioners stayed up to watch.

'And behold the air was filled with the rushing and glistening wings of angels who took the stones of the church and carried them over the water. As they did so the night winds bore back the chant to the onlookers. Over the mere! Over the mere!' The word 'mere' has several interpretations, including 'lake', 'wood' or 'boundary of the wood'. The church was built on the present site, selected by the angels and the village was originally named Uddy-mere.

It is believed that the main road which runs through the village is part of a Roman road which ran from Rye to Uckfield in mid-Sussex.

Udimore, along with Brede, formed the Hundred of Gostrow. Hundreds were districts initiated in the 10th century which may have gained their name from the fact that they provided 100 warriors each or constituted 100 families and their purpose was to administer local government.

After Saxon occupation, the Normans assessed the village in 1086, when it was named in the Domesday survey as Babinrerode.

Parts of the present parish church of St Mary date from the 11th century. It was rebuilt in 1220 and there have been many alterations since. In the beautiful churchyard is the grave of artist W Symons, who was responsible for the mosaics in Westminster Cathedral and inside the church the ornate Jacobean-style pulpit was carved by parishioner Kate Papillon, when she was 18. She died in 1973, aged 89. The impressive Royal Arms of George III, date from 1772 and were restored by the Canterbury School of Art.

The font dates from the 18th century and is a clever forgery. It is made of wood which, according to ancient ecclesiastical rulings, was not allowed. The parish officials at Udimore, for reasons known only to them, but possibly economic, painted a wooden pudding bowl with a stone covering outside and lead paint inside to give the desired effect. It was restored in 1969, a portion of wood left exposed to show the deceit!

The Manor House known as Court Lodge once adjoined the church. It had

St Mary's and Court Lodge

been owned by the Etchingham family since the 12th century. King Edward I stayed there and, in 1350, Edward III, when he reviewed the English fleet prior to the Battle of Winchelsea, when the Spanish were defeated. Queen Eleanor viewed the proceedings from the heights of Udimore. The house was rebuilt in Tudor times but later fell into disrepair and was dismantled in 1912 and re-erected in Groombridge, Kent, where it remains today. Surrounding the buildings which now occupy the site can be seen the remains of part of the 13th century moat which circled the original property.

Its close proximity to the sea made Udimore an obvious place for smuggling. Members of the Whiteman and Miller families gained an infamous entry into village history while pursuing the illicit trade. After several bloody skirmishes with Customs men, Spencer Whiteman and two of the Miller family were arrested and committed for trial at the Old Bailey, where they were sentenced to death. However, this was commuted and they were transported to Tasmania.

The old school building, built in the late 1800s on the narrow Udimore to Winchelsea road, has taken on a new role in the life of the village. It now houses workshop units, run by local businesses. The former Methodist Church has also been adapted for a different use and is now occupied by a joinery company.

The King's Head public house was once used for parish meetings in the early 1800s. The beer was supplied courtesy of the rates! Udimore's second pub is the Plough.

On the high point as the B2089 approaches Rye, a beacon stands beside the road. This was one of hundreds lit across the country in 1988 to mark the 400th anniversary of the defeat of the Armada. At this point it is worth stopping and taking in the magnificent view across to Rye and the sea.

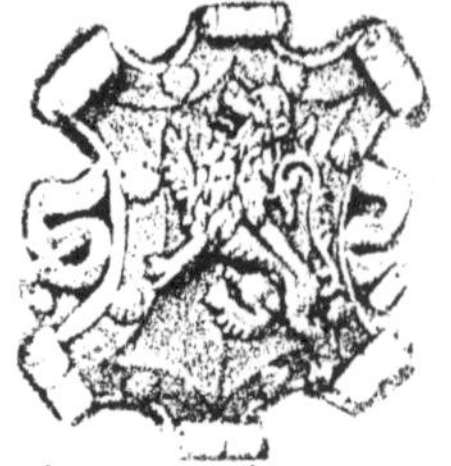

Brede

On leaving the hamlet of Broad Oak at the crossroads, the A28 continues on to Brede, 'the village on the hill'.

Around the year 1030, King Canute, under the scheming influence of his wife, the Norman princess Emma, gave the Manor of Brede, which included a large part of Hastings, to the Abbey of Fecamp, so marking the beginning of the Norman infiltration.

Brede was once an important iron-making centre. Iron-making began there during the reign of Elizabeth I and later guns were supplied from the Brede Furnace to the Parliamentarian armies during the Civil War. To more peaceful ends the furnace produced many fine firebacks.

Iron working ceased in the late 1700s and the Brede Furnace was converted to gunpowder mills. Three severe explosions took place between the years 1778 and 1808, the last one wrecking the whole of the mills and buildings, when two men and a child were blown to pieces. It was reported that debris was scattered as far as 12 miles away.

The furnace and gunpowder works were situated between Brede and Sedlescombe, on the site of the Powdermill Reservoir, which today supplies water to neighbouring Hastings. It is an area much favoured by walkers.

From as early as 1405 until 1892 Brede also had a thriving pottery industry and many fine examples can be seen in Hastings Museum.

For over 900 years a church has stood at the top of Brede Hill, overlooking the Brede Valley. Some of the 11th century building remains but many additions were made up until the 16th century. Today the Church of St George, one of the finest in Sussex, has many attractions, including a 17th century alms box and chest and a carved Madonna by the writer, artist and cousin of Sir Winston Churchill, Clare Sheridan, who once lived locally and is buried in the churchyard. The Madonna is dedicated to her son and was carved from an oak which grew on her estate. The Stations of the Cross are by Sir Thomas Monnington, former president of the Royal Academy.

But pride of place is the beautiful Lady Chapel, where under the great south window, stands the altar tomb of Sir Goddard Oxenbridge, 'the Brede Giant', erected in 1537. History tells us that he was a good, honest man and a great benefactor to the church, who was knighted by King Henry VIII in 1509. But legend has painted a far different picture. For centuries the tale has circulated of Sir Goddard being a fearsome ogre who roamed the

The tomb of Sir Goddard Oxenbridge

countryside carrying off young children and devouring them. The legend goes on to say how he was eventually trapped by the children of Sussex and sawn in two. His ghost is now said to haunt Groaning Bridge, in Stubbs Lane.

The origin of the legend probably derives from a taunt and is a reflection of the bitter religious feuds, which were rife in Sussex in those times. This particular cannibalism legend is peculiar to this part of the country.

Sir Goddard's daughter, Elizabeth, who later became Lady Tirwhitt, was lady-in-waiting to Queen Katherine Parr and was in attendance on the Queen at the time of her fatal illness at Sudely Castle. She was later granted custody of the Princess Elizabeth and made responsible for the future queen's education after the disgrace of the princess's former tutor Katherine Ashley. In 1574 Lady Tirwhitt published a prayer book, a copy of which was presented to Queen Elizabeth, who wore it constantly, suspended by a chain from her waist.

The Oxenbridge family home was nearby Brede Place, formerly known as Forde Place, now a private residence and not open to the public. Brede Place, once described by the architect Lutyens as 'the most interesting inhabited house in England', was also once the home of Clare Sheridan and earlier Stephen Crane, the American author of 'The Red Badge of Courage'. During his occupancy many famous people from the world of literature were regular visitors including H G Wells and Henry James.

In the churchyard of St George's is a small oak cross, marked simply 'Damaris' which causes bewilderment to many visitors. Damaris Richardson was an orphan girl who grew into a beautiful young woman and fell hopelessly in love with Lewis Smith, who lived in Church House in the 1850s. His parents objected to the liaison and forbade it as they considered Damaris's position to be inferior to their son's. The engagement was broken off and Damaris died of a broken heart at the age of 22 and was buried on September 4, 1856 in an unmarked grave close to the spot where the lovers regularly met.

Some years later a gentleman from out of the district, who had been a school acquaintance of Damaris, asked the rector of her whereabouts. When told the tragic story he ordered that the oak cross we see today be placed on the grave.

Damaris's fiancée Lewis Smith never married. He lived at Church House all his life, became a recluse and died there in 1896, aged 65.

From the high point behind the church, glorious views can be enjoyed across the beautiful Brede Valley.

It is said the author J M Barrie based his character Captain Hook on the exploits of a former rector of Brede Church, the Rev William Maher, who supposedly led a double life, combining his clerical duties with that of smuggling. The story is well documented in the ancient Red Lion Inn, which stands opposite the church.

The Red Lion takes its name and sign from the Oxenbridge arms and is mentioned in the Letters and Papers of Henry VIII and a hundred years ago was the headquarters of the illicit Sussex smuggling trade.

After descending the steep hill and crossing the narrow bridge over the River Brede, it is worth pondering that the river was once a tidal arm of the sea and up until the 1930s, barges brought coal and provisions from Rye, some eight miles distant to a wharf at the bridge.

Westfield

The last village before the A28 returns to Hastings is the former iron-smelting village of Westfield. Settlement began in Saxon times and according to the Domesday Book, the Manor of Westwell was given to the Count of Eu, after the Norman Conquest.

There are several historic buildings in the village, including the former forge, Old School House, and the fine Norman church of St John the Baptist. The two public houses serving the village are The Plough and The New Inn.

The church stands on the site of a much earlier Saxon place of worship and the lower portion of the tower dates from that period. It was extended during Norman times and further additions have been made since.

In 1251 the monks of Battle Abbey were given responsibility for the Parish of Westfield by the Bishop of Chichester and at this time the chancel was extended eastwards. The two 'squints' were cut through the chancel arch wall when it was found the congregation could not see the proceedings at the altar. Other interesting features are the south door, dated 1542, the old carved oak pulpit with sounding board and the high font with antique cover.

Westfield's major modern attraction is the vineyard, created by a local engineer, which produced its first vintage in 1976. Westfield was put on the map when much media attention was given to the vineyard, as it produced the classic 'coals to Newcastle' story by becoming one of the first English vineyards to export wine to France. Many awards have been won for the sparkling wine produced there.

The modern winery sits in 21 acres of vineyard and various types of white and limited amounts of red wine are produced. The vineyard, taught by a French expert, even produces an English version of champagne, made from the same type of grapes and using traditional French champenoise methods.

The wines are on sale and advice is given on planting your own vineyard. There are also trails to follow and group tours can be made by arrangement.